Unchained Russia

AMERICANS IN REVOLUTIONARY RUSSIA

Vol. 1
Albert Rhys Williams, *Through the Russian Revolution*,
edited by William Benton Whisenhunt (2016)

Vol. 2
Princess Julia Cantacuzène, Countess Spéransky, née Grant, *Russian People: Revolutionary Recollections*, edited by Norman E. Saul (2016)

Vol. 3
Ernest Poole, *The Village: Russian Impressions*, edited by Norman E. Saul (2017)

Vol. 4
John Reed, *Ten Days That Shook the World*, edited by William Benton Whisenhunt (2017)

Vol. 5
Louise Bryant, *Six Red Months in Russia*, edited by Lee A. Farrow (2017)

Vol. 6
Edward Alsworth Ross, *Russia in Upheaval*, edited by Rex A. Wade (2017)

Vol. 7
Donald Thompson, *Donald Thompson in Russia*, edited by David H. Mould (2017)

Vol. 8
Arthur Bullard, *The Russian Pendulum: Autocracy—Democracy—Bolshevism*,
edited by David W. McFadden (2019)

Vol. 9
David Francis, *Russia from the American Embassy*, edited by Vladimir V. Noskov (2019)

Vol. 10
Pauline S. Crosley, *Intimate Letters from Petrograd*, edited by Lee A. Farrow (2019)

Vol. 11
Madeleine Z. Doty, *"The Bolshevik Revolution Had Descended on Me": Madeleine Z. Doty's Russian Revolution*, edited by Julia L. Mickenberg (2019)

Vol. 12
John R. Mott, *the American YMCA, and Revolutionary Russia*,
edited by Matthew Lee Miller (2020)

Vol. 13
Carl W. Ackerman, *Trailing the Bolsheviki: Twelve Thousand Miles with the Allies in Siberia*, edited by Ivan Kurilla (2020)

Vol. 14
Malcolm C. Grow, *Surgeon Grow: An American in the Russian Fighting*,
edited by Laurie S. Stoff (2021)

Series General Editors: Norman E. Saul and William Benton Whisenhunt

Unchained Russia

Charles Edward Russell

Edited and Introduction by
Rex A. Wade

ANTHEM PRESS

Anthem Press
An imprint of Wimbledon Publishing Company
www.anthempress.com

First published by Slavica Publishers, Indiana University, USA, 2021

This edition first published in UK and USA 2026
by ANTHEM PRESS
75–76 Blackfriars Road, London SE1 8HA, UK
or PO Box 9779, London SW19 7ZG, UK
and
244 Madison Ave #116, New York, NY 10016, USA

Copyright © 2026 Rex A. Wade editorial matter and selection;
individual chapters © individual contributors

The moral right of the authors has been asserted.

All rights reserved. Without limiting the rights under copyright reserved above,
no part of this publication may be reproduced, stored or introduced into
a retrieval system, or transmitted, in any form or by any means
(electronic, mechanical, photocopying, recording or otherwise),
without the prior written permission of both the copyright
owner and the above publisher of this book.

British Library Cataloguing-in-Publication Data
A catalogue record for this book is available from the British Library.

Library of Congress Cataloging-in-Publication Data: 2025945114

ISBN-13: 978-1-83999-756-3(Hbk)
ISBN-10: 1-83999-756-7 (Hbk)

ISBN-13: 978-1-83999-757-0(Pbk)
ISBN-10: 1-83999-757-5(Pbk)

Cover design: Tracey Theriault

This title is also available as an eBook.

Contents

Rex A. Wade

    Editor's Introduction ix

Unchained Russia

I. New Russia and "the Tsar's War" 3

II. The Real Propulsion and the Real Hope 21

III. Two Aspects of the New Faith 44

IV. The Old Regime and Its Fruitage 56

V. A Broken Down Railroad and What Came of It 70

VI. The Part Played by Russian Women 86

VII. The Peasant 97

VIII. The Bolshevik 112

IX. The Influence of Manners and Morals 128

Index 143

Editor's Introduction
Rex A. Wade

A popular revolt broke out in Petrograd, Russia, on February 23–27, 1917. It grew rapidly into a full revolution that overthrew the tsarist monarchy, replacing it by a Provisional Government that was officially created a few weeks later on March 2. The United States ambassador to Russia, David R. Francis, successfully pushed his government to be the first state to recognize the new regime diplomatically, which it did on March 9 (22).[1] This quickly led President Woodrow Wilson to take various steps to facilitate the Russian war effort. One of these was the creation of a special delegation to go to Russia to study the situation there and report back. Recognizing the importance of Russian socialists in the politics of the time, he realized that having a prominent American socialist in the group—even a moderate one—could be useful. Charles Edward Russell was an attractive choice. While famous as a leftist, socialist, activist, and author, in early 1917 he emerged among American socialists as a major supporter of the American war effort, something many American socialists of the time opposed.

Russell was a major intellectual figure and writer in the late nineteenth and early twentieth century America. He was a journalist, newspaper editor, political activist, and author of many books and articles about issues of the time. His was a very diverse but also very active life. His writing on social and economic issues made him famous as one of the "muckrakers" of the time, as Theodore Roosevelt called them. He became active in the American socialist movement and was a prominent member of the American socialist party from 1908 to 1917, including being a socialist candidate in New York four times for either state governor or US senator. In 1917, however, he was one of the socialists thrown out of the party for supporting American entry into the war, which then opened another avenue of notable activity, as we will see in this book.

---

[1] I have changed all the dating from the Gregorian calendar that he used to the Julian calendar—the calendar in use in Russia in 1917. The latter, thirteen days behind the former, was still in use in 1917 Russia, and is increasingly used in most writing today about the Russian Revolution of 1917. One result is that the original 1917 revolution is known as both the February Revolution and the March Revolution, and the Bolshevik acquisition of power is known as both the October Revolution and the November Revolution in writings by Americans and other Westerners, depending on the calendar they used. The Bolshevik regime changed the Russian calendar to the Gregorian one in early 1917.

He later won the Pulitzer Prize for his 1928 book *The American Orchestra and Theodore Thomas*, the only Pulitzer Prize ever awarded for the biography of a musician! Russell was one of the founders, an officer, and a lifetime member of the National Association for the Advancement of Colored People, even though he was white, and was given notable praise by it at his death in 1941. He was a fascinating, important figure, famous in his time in many ways.[2]

Born and raised in Davenport, Iowa, Russell worked in the local newspaper under his father, and then finally moved to New York City in 1886. He quickly built a notable reputation, partly based on innovative, investigative reporting about political and social issues. He also became a famous reform advocate. His pre-1917 writing became especially famous after his investigation of New York City's Trinity Church's corruption as a slum landlord, but he also wrote about railroad abuses, stockyard workers, and other topics that made his reputation as a major reformer with socialist leanings, although he was not among the more radical socialists of the time. Therefore, President Woodrow Wilson could add him as the "leftist" in the official American delegation to Russia in 1917. His experience there had a big impact, leading to the production of this book, and it also led to other Russia-related activities, including his participation in a 1917 American film about the revolution, *The Fall of the Romanoffs*.[3] After his involvement in Russia ended, he continued to be politically active and the author of numerous books and articles on a wide range of topics. Despite often calling himself and being called by others a socialist, and participating in a socialist party, he was not so much opposed to capitalism as much as to the extreme concentration of wealth and the resulting power of only a few. His focus was on creating more equal opportunity for everyone.

Russell's *Unchained Russia* book told readers a great deal about Russia in mid-1917. He starts by stating that the people of the US and Russia did not understand each other at that time, a theme that was correct and runs throughout the book. He stresses immediately, page one, that the revolution was economic as well as political, which reflected both a better-than-normal understanding of the revolution in 1917 and his own political-economic and pro-labor background. It also gave him an opportunity

---

[2] Many authors and works, on many subjects, reference Russell's writing. Two particularly relevant ones for our subject, but very different in size, might be mentioned. One is Robert Miraldi, *The Pen is Mightier: The Muckraking Life of Charles Edward Russell* (New York: Palgrave Macmillan, 2003), which speaks about the central part of his life from 1889, when he was 29, to 1918, when he was still only 59, with many years yet to live and write. Another especially informative document is a more recent (2020), lengthy Wikipedia piece, "Charles Edward Russell," https://en.wikipedia.org/wiki/Charles_Edward_Russell. In addition to a good biographical essay, it identifies thirty-two of his books, gives a long list of selected articles, names the one 1917 film that he participated in, and provides a References and a Sources section. Miraldi provides the same list of books and a year by year list of magazine articles.

[3] A remarkable early film which started in 1917 and had revised versions following that.

to emphasize the importance of sweeping political change and social-economic reform in the US as well as in Russia. However, he notes that when many Americans saw that what was happening in Russia was social-economic change as well as basic political democracy, "instinctively we shied away."[4] The opening pages make clear his own relative political and economic radicalism in the US at that time, which, as we have noted, had played a role in his selection to be on the American delegation.

The image of revolutionary Russia that he communicated was a complex, somewhat contradictory one. Early, in Chapter I, he lays out the popular foreign image of drunken peasants and how that shaped our attitude as the revolution progressed and influenced foreign newspaper accounts. He notes, however, that Russians had achieved much social and economic change already, but that "our" newspapers focused more on the drunken peasants story than on what ordinary Russians were achieving. We were profoundly misinformed, he argues. He blames that image not on the American correspondents who were there, but on German press agents deliberately developing false stories that seemed believable. This stress on the role of German agents in various events runs for several pages here and is repeated from time to time, and perhaps is the book's chief weakness. It should be largely ignored by modern readers except as an example of widespread American thought of the times, especially after our entry into the war. However, Russell does assert with significant accuracy the sacredness of the revolution to ordinary Russians of the time and recognizes that so many saw it as the beginning of a new era for them, and for humanity generally, and that the new order should be based on workers and peasants. He agreed! He does criticize, again correctly, that the Allied governments did not generally recognize that belief.

Russell notes early on that the real power in Russia rested with the Soviets, first the Petrograd Soviet and then its later reconstructions, including the first All-Russian Congress of Soviets of Workers' and Soldiers' Deputies on July 1–3 (Russian calendar), which he observed. Indeed, he apparently met frequently with the Russian moderate socialists who, in effect, controlled the Russian government and policies in mid-1917, many of whom are rarely mentioned in Western books written at the same time he wrote his, and even more rarely after the Bolsheviks seized power and civil war broke out. He talked with important Soviet leaders of 1917, such as Irakli Tsereteli, Nikolai Chkheidze, and Mikhail Skobelev, among others, and even with the recently arrived but rapidly rising Leon Trotsky.[5] He gives us good, brief accounts of these people, as this Americans in Revolutionary Russia series of books generally does—a picture

---

[4] Charles Edward Russell, *Unchained Russia* (New York: D. Appleton, 1918), 3.

[5] Tsereteli, Chkheidze, and Skobelev were especially important leaders from March to October 1917, and some might say they actually governed Russia at the time Russell was there— Chkheidze and Tsereteli through their leadership of the Petrograd Soviet, Skobelev in his role as one of the Soviet and government leaders. Trotsky had just returned from exile in the United States and was at the beginning of his rise to effective leadership of the radical left,

of what Russia and its revolution seemed to be at the time, not the kind of heavily revised versions that followed later. At the same time, he had a high admiration for ordinary Russians and a belief that the Soviets could create a complete democracy in Russia, a democracy stripped down to its plainest terms and accepted unflinchingly.

He was very struck by important symbols of revolution and a changed world. This comes up regularly, such as in his description of the Congress of Soviets, which he had observed. He is not just describing a Russian event, however, but giving a vision of a new world. Indeed, he devotes significant space to celebrating the Russian Revolution not only as a major change for Russia, but also as a new symbol of worldwide change. That included his early notation of the symbolism of the red flag adopted in 1917 Russia, significantly before the Bolsheviks took over and used it as theirs. Indeed, much of the book reflects the Russian and Western optimism of the time that a turn from a horrendous old regime toward a better new world had begun. That fit with the perspectives, even reality, of 1917. Being aware of that is useful to a modern reader in that it reflects a very popular belief at the time, especially in the US after our entry into the war.

He also dwells on and repeats the most negative depictions of tsarist officials. He gives a very negative picture of the old regime, and especially the behavior of officials and military officers. His account of the tsarist police in Chapter IV is perhaps a bit exaggerated, but it does reflect a reality that existed, although he probably overstates the ability and extent of the old police.

Russell spent railroad time in Siberia and in other parts of the countryside, and he gives interesting descriptions of ordinary Russians that he met along the way. Indeed, his discussion of railroads, especially the Trans-Siberian in Chapter V, is overall quite good, noting that in some respects the Russian railroads were better than the American ones and in other ways were worse than American ones, and why. He gives a good account of the railway problems and issues, reflecting the American concern about the need for the railroads in the Russian war effort. The US put significant effort into keeping the railroads working, in part because it was essential to getting US supplies and support to the Russian government and its war effort. His travel across Russia—from the Pacific to Petrograd and Moscow and then back again—also provided him some interesting possibilities for descriptions of rural Russia. He even gives a good description of Lake Baikal when frozen over in winter and the issues that caused, something that also was of importance to the US. He would have learned that from the Russians there, given that he was in the Lake Baikal region in summer, not winter.

Russell gives a full chapter to women and stresses the role they played. He, like most visitors who wrote, had a great interest in the subject of the Provisional Gov-

---

soon to be head of the Petrograd Soviet and then a top leader of the Bolshevik government at the time Russell wrote this book.

ernment giving women universal and equal voting rights, making Russia the first major power to do that. He not only focused on women in the February Revolution and certain significant ones such as "Mother Catherine" and Maria Spiridonova, but also on women who participated in various meetings, worked on various jobs (such as railroads), and helped reshape society generally. He adds to that a section on women's military service, especially Maria Botchkareva and the newly created women's battalions, a subject that aroused the interest of many visitors.

In the final two chapters he turns increasingly to the Bolsheviks, who were not yet in power when he was there, but were by the time he returned home and wrote the book, which came out in early 1918. These would have been very important topics for his readers. His chapter on Bolsheviks gives an interesting, and reasonably good, account of the early Western attitude toward Bolsheviks. He viewed the Bolsheviks' success as perhaps inevitable in the Russia of the time: "Instead of an abnormal product the Bolshevik was in Russia the most natural fruitage" of the old regime.[6] Few people would have used that terminology, perhaps, but it fit with his view of the Bolsheviks as a passing phenomenon. Actually, it is a pretty good reflection of the initial optimism of many at the time that the Bolshevik seizure of power was a temporary thing. Although he disliked the Bolsheviks and their seizure of power, he retained confidence that broader democracy would prevail.

Overall, he writes a quite optimistic view of the revolution, not only as an event in and of itself, but for the future of world politics. Indeed, he argues, reflecting both his admiration for the revolution and his own political hopes for significant change in the United States, that "the Russian Revolutionists had shot far beyond political democracy; they aimed at industrial democracy no less."[7]

Perhaps I should close this introduction with a few notes about my editing, as I tried to make it more readable in our times. I have changed all the dating from the Gregorian calendar that he used to the Julian calendar, the one in use in Russia in 1917, as mentioned in a footnote earlier. The other major revision is that I changed his frequent use of the word "slavery" to "serfdom," which is what had existed in Russia. Serfdom did impose restrictions on peasants, but they also were partially free and certainly were not slaves in the American sense. Going back and forth between the two terms was common for foreigners, especially Americans writing at that time. I also changed his use of the word "czar" (widely used at the time in the West) to the more accurate and modern spelling "tsar." He refers to Bloody Sunday in 1905 Russia as Bloody Monday, and I have changed all of those. He may be pulling the term from a nineteenth century American event known as Bloody Monday. Once in a while I add a word in parentheses to make the sentence or subject clearer. Lastly,

---

[6] Russell, *Unchained Russia*, 253.

[7] Ibid., 2–3.

I owe a huge thanks to Ben Whisenhunt and to Anne Marie Watkins for their enormous help in preparing this book.

Suggested Further Reading

Badcock, Sarah. *Politics and the People in Revolutionary Russia: A Provincial History*. Cambridge: Cambridge University Press, 2007.

Browder, Robert Paul, and Alexander F. Kerensky. *The Russian Provisional Government, 1917: Documents*. 3 vols. Stanford: Stanford University Press, 1961.

Figes, Orlando, and Boris Kolonitskii. *Interpreting the Russian Revolution: The Language and Symbols of 1917*. New Haven, CT: Yale University Pres, 1999.

Galili, Ziva. *The Menshevik Leaders in the Russian Revolution: Social Realities and Political Strategies*. Princeton, NJ: Princeton University Press, 1989.

Hasegawa, Tsuyoshi. *Crime and Punishment in the Russian Revolution: Mob Justice and Police in Petrograd*. Cambridge, MA: Harvard University Press, 2017.

Hickey, Michael C., ed. *Competing Voices from the Russian Revolution*. Santa Barbara, CA: ABC-CLIO, 2011.

Koenker, Diane, and William G. Rosenberg. *Strikes and Revolution in Russia, 1917*. Princeton, NJ: Princeton University Press, 1989.

Miraldi, Robert. *The Pen is Mightier: The Muckraking Life of Charles Edward Russell*. New York: Palgrave, 2001.

Rabinowitch, Alexander. *The Bolsheviks Come to Power: The Revolution of 1917 in Petrograd*. New York: Newton, 1976.

Raleigh, Donald. *Revolution on the Volga: 1917 in Saratov*. Ithaca, NY: Cornell University Press, 1986.

Read, Christopher. *From Tsar to Soviets: The Russian People and Their Revolution*. New York: Oxford University Press, 1996.

Rendle, Mathew. *Defenders of the Motherland: The Tsarist Elite in Revolutionary Russia*. Oxford: Oxford University Press, 2010.

Revolutionary Russia 30, no. 1 (June 2017) and no. 2 (December 2017).

Rosenberg, William. *Liberals in the Russian Revolution: The Constitutional Democratic Party, 1917–1921*. Princeton, NJ: Princeton University Press, 1974.

"Russell, Charles Edward." Wikipedia, August 24, 2020, https://en.wikipedia.org/wiki/Charles_Edward_Russell.

Russia's Great War and Revolution. 7 vols. Bloomington, IN: Slavica.

Saul, Norman. *War and Revolution: The United States and Russia, 1914–1921*. Lawrence: University of Kansas, 2001.

Smith, S. A. *Red Petrograd: Revolution in the Factories*. Cambridge: Cambridge University Press, 1983.

Steinberg, Mark D. *Voices of Revolution, 1917*. New Haven, CT: Yale University Press, 2001.

Swain, Geoffrey. *A Short History of the Russian Revolution*. London: I. B. Tauris, 2017.

Thatcher, Ian D., ed. *Reinterpreting Revolutionary Russia: Essays in Honour of James D. White*. New York: Palgrave-Macmillan, 2006.

Wade, Rex A. "The Revolution at One Hundred: Issues and Trends in the English Language Historiography of the Russian Revolution of 1917." *Journal of Russian History and Historiography* 9, no. 1 (2016): 9–38.

———. *The Russian Revolution, 1917*. 3rd ed. Cambridge: Cambridge University Press, 2017.

———. *The Russian Search for Peace, February–October 1917*. Stanford: Stanford University Press, 1969.

Wildman, Allan K. *The End of the Russian Imperial Army*. 2 vols. Princeton, NJ: Princeton University Press, 1980–87.

UNCHAINED RUSSIA

BY

CHARLES EDWARD RUSSELL

MEMBER OF THE AMERICAN SPECIAL DIPLOMATIC MISSION TO RUSSIA IN 1917;
AUTHOR OF "BUSINESS: THE HEART OF THE NATION,"
"THOMAS CHATTERTON: THE MARVELOUS BOY,"
"THESE SHIFTING SCENES," "THE STORY OF
WENDELL PHILLIPS," ETC.

D. APPLETON AND COMPANY

NEW YORK, LONDON

1918

Chapter I
New Russia and "the Tsar's War"

To the last syllable of recorded time, mankind is likely to have cause to lament that in the years 1917 and 1918 the people of the United States did not understand the people of Russia and the people of Russia did not understand the people of the United States.

As to the people of the United States, our share of the understanding was partly natural and partly manufactured: partly sheer distance from the stage and partly inattention and mental laziness.

The great Russian Revolution of February, 1917, was economic and political. We persisted in accepting it as only political. To get rid of the Tsar and political absolutism, to have done with the absurd medieval trappings of monarchy, to set up a representative republic like our own: these were objects we could well understand and sympathize with. To reform, in the interest of all mankind, the existing social system; to abolish poverty; to secure for the masses every possible chance for culture and comfort; to end the modern world's sottish conditions of too much and too little: these were objects that seemed to us dreamy, anarchistic or insane. With the startling news of the Revolution we grasped rejoicingly the first series of objects; the Tsar was gone, the old hateful tyranny was no more, blessed be the day! But when word came of the second series of objects we chilled rapidly, then looked askance, then began to turn upon the whole manifestation a face of frowning reproof.[1]

This was nothing to be wondered at. The United States had, for the time being, stopped on a dead center in its democratic Revolution. It had ceased, or apparently ceased, to go ahead democratically, and some persons of limited vision even thought it was floating backward. A lapse of this kind takes place in the story of every republic. Having won political freedom we were for the time content to think there was nothing more to be done and to roll about where we were, inert socially and threatened with fatty degeneration morally. But the Russian Revolutionists had shot far beyond political democracy; they aimed at industrial democracy no less. All the years when they were so bravely in the darkness struggling for freedom and light, carrying on their secret propaganda, making infinite sacrifices for the sake of an ideal, walking always under the shadow of a horrible fate, those unsung heroes of Russia that have gone by the thousands to graves, were working toward this two-fold aim. Political freedom

---

[1] The reference here is to the October (Bolshevik) Revolution.

was well, it was very well; but it was well chiefly because it offered a means by which the masses of men that toil could secure a larger share of the wealth their toil created. Freedom meant a world freed from the blight of kings and freed no less from the blight of an industrial system that condemned nine men in every ten to poverty; a world with no more despots and no more slums.

To oust the old Russian political system, blood-dripping and odious, was the necessary beginning. We, still shackled more or less to another century and to the petrifactions of a philosophy good in its day but now grown rusty as a stage coach, thought it was an end, and when we began to see there was another program instinctively we shied away.

As a matter of fact, the new program was, at first, nothing really alarming. The dominant thought in Russia was not then that the change could be effected overnight. Almost in an hour, the nation passed from an archaic and criminal tyranny to a democracy where, for a time, at least, the majority ruled. The majority had never accepted the doctrines of those that wished to pull up everything by the roots or build from clouds the domes of glittering Utopia. Utopia they were determined to have some day, if you like so to call it, but not being insane they did not think they could get it with an incantation.

Here, then, is the first point, that if the people of the United States had understood this reasoning majority and had manifested sympathy with it, and if at the same time there had been an adequate effort to counter-attack the German propaganda on Russian soil, we should have had a different story to tell of the developments of the great war. For if Russia had kept steadfast to the cause of the Allies the war would have ended in 1917 and the safety of democracy would have been truly assured.

As to the manufactured part of the American misunderstanding of Russia, that on our side was only in a small way malicious or prepensive. We must remember that at our best we started off on the wrong foot about Russia. Those of us that had found any leisure for such studies had inflexible notions drawn from the Russian novels we had read and the works of English travelers we had labored through, and we felt that our own gained knowledge we would profane if we did not hold to the mental images won at such a cost. We knew that Russia was a country of dense ignorance, primitive conditions, bad roads, dull peasants and ever flowing vodka. We knew well the typical Russian of the upper class, polished, handsome, witty, a little dangerous if a man, romantically alluring if a woman, supporting, of course, this system of imperial despotism; but after all, what could you expect? The Russian people were so ignorant and so degraded, the Nihilists were so violent—plainly there could be no democracy in such a country.[2]

---

[2] Nihilism was a movement that emerged in the nineteenth century party advocating revolution using terrorism and assassination. It rejected all authority. In Russia it faded for a period and then arose again during 1917. There were multiple anarchist parties (cooperation was not a feature of anarchism in 1917) which represented a small but very assertive movement. This

We thought, too, sometimes of the peasant, stupidly good-natured, bestial, loutish, unkempt and unwashed, having but a vestige of a mind and drunk most of the time. In mentally conjured pictures we saw him standing rammishly about as he always stood in the pages of our favorite novels; we had mind upon his long tangled hair, his long sprawling beard, his trousers in his great boots, his belt and strange tunic instead of the coat and collar of civilization; and the whole of him spelled to us only a figure of sodden imbecility. And he and his kind made up 75 per cent of the population! What a country! Who could have hope of it?

After 1914, when a decree of the Tsar evicted the vodka demon from his native land, this accepted picture of ours was somewhat marred. If there was no vodka the peasant class could not be drunk all the time. Still we clung resolutely to what was left, and as to the drunkenness contrived to think that if there was no vodka there must be something else. Beer, if taken in sufficient quantities, would, it was believed, produce intoxication. Perhaps the Tsar's decree did not include beer, and the peasant might still be conscientiously faithful to a picture of him limned by so many able pens that no reading people could be expected to give it up.

And now a population of which the great majority were of this order had been suddenly endowed with democracy, a benefaction of which necessarily it could know nothing, and being so endowed it was minded to change a social structure sanctified with the approval of all the old established and successful nations, including both democracies and near-democracies! Under these conditions it was but natural that we should feel first alarm and then aversion.

But so far as the great mass of the people were concerned, those that had never read Russian novels, that had never unraveled the sour and intorted [twisted] criticisms of travelers, nor suspected there could be anything admirable about a despotism steeped in blood and corruption, for them the making of misunderstanding proceeded upon a gigantic scale in the columns of the daily press. Unintentionally, no doubt of that, at least at this end of the line. It was not the American editor's fault that day by day he printed in his news columns matter about Russia that poisoned the minds and perverted the judgments of his readers. He had not the slightest suspicion of the thimble-rigging of which he was the victim. There seems to be no help for these things and no reason to find fault with the sure by-product of modern commerce. The business of the newspaper was to furnish its readers with "good stories." Everything relating to Russia that indicated violence, conflict, riot, any manifested tendency to uproot and destroy, was naturally a "good story"; it had the requisite of action, the sauce without which any news article is to our taste but flat and juiceless.

There was no "good story" in the tame events of government's daily routine, in the worthy things the new democracy achieved, in its astonishing success in main-

---

paragraph presents a negative view of Russia—that he is attributing to Western thought—as an erroneous one.

taining order, in its efforts to establish universal education and universal suffrage, to extend and safeguard the rights of the people, to institute a system of justice, actual and uncorrupted, where none had been before, to meet such problems as had never confronted any other newly launched nation in the history of the world, to straighten the tangles left by the Tsar's incomparable band of thieves and bunglers. No such matter would lay touch upon the ganglions of any reader's imagination; why, therefore, should they be printed? But the "good stories," though doubtless very good, convinced a public already bent to such a judgment that Russia was in a state of utter chaos, liberty had become merely license, and the return of despotism in some shape or other was inevitable. At a time when Petrograd was one of the most orderly cities in the world, the opera bouffe performances of a little band of notoriety-seeking Anarchists were assumed to mean universal ruin and desolation; an insignificant change in an always insignificant cabinet was interpreted as the forerunner of a Napoleon and a new form of empire; any procession of workingmen heralded barricades in the streets and firing from the house tops.

It is not to be denied that we assisted these processes with an open-mouthed and apparently unfailing credulity. The weirdest achievements of romantic fancy looked but pale compared with some of the stories cabled from Stockholm and Copenhagen, Christiania and Amsterdam, purporting to give news of Russia; but none of them seemed too hectic for our naive faith. We read one day a narrative that anyone so much as glancing at a map would see was not merely incredible but impossible, and the next day read another equally strange but exactly reversing the first, and apparently we not only believed both but were ready the next day for a third flight of fancy inconsistent with either of the others. The psychology of the public's seeming readiness to take for true any morbid invention that bears a foreign date line is beyond explanation. If we were to learn by word of mouth the self-same tale we sometimes read in the foreign despatches we should not be in the least danger of believing it; once cast into type with the name of a European city tagged to it, and it seems to have the authority of holy writ. A great good fortune that befell this country was the high character and extraordinary ability of the American newspaper correspondents in Russia at this time. All were of long experience and cool judgment, and two, Arnot Dosch Fleurot and William G. Shepherd, had distinguished themselves by the most brilliant war reporting the conflict had brought forth anywhere.[3] But the good correspondents in Petrograd could not stem the tide of misrepresentation that went forth for the reason that most of it was concocted outside of Russia. It was for this that the neutral capitals of Europe swarmed with German press agents. They knew ways to poison the news while it was in transit; they knew how to start a story, to give to it all the appearance of verity, to launch it in circles that were above the least suspicion and

---

[3] Fleurot and Shepherd were two famous American World War I journalists who went into Russia in 1917.

thus to send it on its way carrying concealed between its lines the deadly mandragora [a deadly plant].[4]

What, for instance, was more simple or more certain than to print in some newspaper they secretly owned a story that purported to be of grave official origin and to pack its words around some cunning assertion that would cause Americans to form a desired opinion about Russia, or Russians to form a desired opinion about America? What could be easier than to flood the sources of news with reports that were half truths, twisted to give a desired impression?

All the conditions, therefore, were perfectly adapted for the beclouding in this country of the real issues involved in the Russian struggle, and, besides the German propaganda, there was another agency that was glad to use them. We must remember there was still left in and about Russia a certain considerable element that most heartily wished to have the Revolution end in failure. Not merely the old reactionary noble class; that was largely shelved or happily overawed. I mean chiefly the great landowners, afflicted with a fear that their possessions were about to be divided among the peasants; many of the manufacturers and men in the financial interest, who looked with quaking terror upon the Revolution's avowed aim of a new basis of division for the products of industry; and (because of a phenomenon familiar to all that know the monarchical capitals of Europe) the socially ambitious in the foreign colony of Petrograd. No doubt many of these believed the wild-eyed tales they set afloat or helped to circulate; self-deception is very easy in such conditions. Be that as it may, through such agencies the mind of America was abused about Russia and two nations that had a great common cause, a common inspiration and a common danger, drifted apart when they should have been bound together in closest cooperation.

But as to the German propaganda, that marvelous institution must always rank in history as one of the greatest achievements of man's wits. Before the war, through its skilled observers here and elsewhere, it had studied, not in vain, the mental operations of the American public and the excellences of the American newspaper. It understood perfectly the valuation and the function of the "good story" and knew how to provide that requisite in Stockholm or any other European center no less than in Washington. Just as certainly as Ambassador von Bernstorff was able by his adroit manipulations to mislead American opinion about the German atrocities and the purposes for which Germany made the war, so easily were the German agents that swarmed in the news centers of continental Europe able to start the stream of "good stories" that landed incessantly upon an able but unsuspecting press.[5] There

---

[4] This is his ongoing anti-German material. It is worth remembering that only a little earlier, in April 1917, the US had entered the war against Germany. Here, and numerous times below, are passages profoundly anti-German, and which exaggerate the German influence in Russia, reflecting the broad belief of the time.

[5] Von Bernstorff was the German ambassador to the United States during World War I and directed extensive anti-Allied sabotage actions before leaving when the US declared war.

was at times a sardonic impudence about their work calculated to take the breath of a casual observer. Perhaps they never excelled in this line their achievement in seizing a fairly well known story of Anatole France's,[6] localizing it in Russia and sending it to America as "news." This seems to me about as far as it is possible to go in this particular field of endeavor, although I admit the ingenuity that on the American election day delivered to every American newspaper a dream story that Germany had been "democratized" to have been more diabolical.

I think it will always seem to the historical investigator in times to come very strange and significant that while other nations from 1871 to 1914 were (under the shadow and menace of Bismarckism) busily developing other instruments of war, the Germans alone paid any attention to the instrument destined to be the most powerful and effective. The British built up the dreadnaught and superdreadnaught battleships; the French devised the world's most efficient artillery; Americans invented and bestowed upon others the submarine, the aeroplane, the best machine guns, the best small arms. Only the Germans turned their minds to the press agency, and by comparison of results that fact would seem to give them some ground for their idea of the German superman.[7]

They had taken seriously to heart the great lesson of Bismarck and the Ems despatch of 1870. If a clever forger with a few strokes of his pen could so influence public opinion that he could precipitate a war, create an empire and steal two provinces, the manipulation of public opinion by whatsoever means had become the great factor in national success, and diligently they applied themselves to the art that Bismarck had indicated.

In any other country the notion of controlled publicity as a practical engine of war would have caused at any time an intellectual tarantella. It was not taught in the text books; neither West Point nor Sandhurst countenanced it. Traditionally and according to all the revered authorities the newspaper was to the making of war an unmitigated nuisance; only the Germans thought of turning it into an adjunct. Twenty years their government spent in patient, diligent, thoughtful effort to bring it to perfection. I saw it in operation in Berlin in 1905 and wrote amazedly of it; but even the colossal machine of 1905, covering the earth, operating in every printed language, able to watch everything from Nova Zembla to the line, from Machias to Far Cathay, was less than the machine that in 1914 poisoned the daily reading and subtly influenced the thinking of millions of earth's inhabitants. On deliberate reflection it will seem clear that this, for practical results, overshadowed all the achievements of

---

[6] Famous French novelist.

[7] Bismarck was the great Prussian/German leader whose policies had unified Germany and made it the great power it was at this time.

a hundred Krupps and another hundred Moltkes.[8] Without it the German people would never have danced after the mad pied piper of world domination and world plunder; without it there might have been no war; without it the United States could never have been kept standing off and on for two years and eight months, an idle spectator of a struggle in which its own existence was at stake. And without it the people of the United States could never have been kept from a sympathetic understanding of Russia and the people of Russia could never have been kept from a sympathetic understanding of the people of the United States.

From the first rifle shot of the Revolution the German propaganda had worked tirelessly to some such end. The economic, financial and influential conquest of Russia was old German strategy. For years Russia had been flooded with German ideas and suggestions no less than with German goods. German capital was developing the industries of Russia; Germans were coming to dominate the Russian banks; insidious, clever campaigning was changing Petrograd into a German city. The imposing German embassy building, one of the largest of the kind in the world, housed an army of directing press and other agents that knew Russia infallibly. At the outbreak of the war the German ambassador withdrew his corporeal presence, but the work he had directed went on without him. A vast network of agents, covering every part of the country, operated a silently working and almost faultless enginery to control public opinion. Beyond doubt these agents knew well enough that the Revolution was close at hand if they did not actually assist in staging it. The instant it broke they knew their best play was to separate Russia from its Allies, and after nine months of incessant work they were able to look upon that end as practically accomplished. All by the skillful use of propaganda. A thousand great guns had no such influence upon the war.

It was a triumph won almost without opposition. Against the enormous German machine so widely dispersed, so cunningly handled, the cause of the Allies[9] went practically unchampioned. I trust it will be perfectly clear that to say this implies no censure and no criticism. Probably no man was to blame that the Russians, beset

---

[8] Gustav Krupp was the most important German industrialist, and Helmeth von Moltke the Younger an important German general.

[9] Russell's note: "It can hardly be necessary but will serve to keep the record quite straight if I recall here the historical fact that the United States did not enter the war and become one of the Allies until almost a month after the Russian Revolution. It is but justice to say that the American Ambassador, Mr. David R. Francis, was the most popular foreigner in Petrograd and his speeches to the Revolutionists are likely to be cherished among the memorials of those troubled days as long as anything man said then shall survive. I have seen his carriage, passing through the streets, stopped by an eager throng that would not cease its cheering nor allow him to proceed until he had stood forth and delivered one of his earnest and sympathetic messages to the Russian people." For David R. Francis's experiences as American ambassador to Russia during the Russian Revolution, see his *Russia from the American Embassy*, ed. Vladimir V. Noskov (Bloomington, IN: Slavica, 2019).

with ingenious falsehoods from Berlin, had never a chance to learn the truth. We must bear always in mind that the situation was new and contradicted all previous experience of the traditional agencies of government. Men are not to be censured if they come slowly and reluctantly to a weapon they have always despised.

There were certain other features of the case that did the Allies' cause no good, although I suppose no one could have changed them. Men that all their lives have believed sincerely in a constitutional monarchy as the best attainable form of human government are not to be expected to warm quickly to a red, radical republic. Men that saw with dismay a near relative of their own monarch rudely hurled from his throne could not be expected to conceal all regret at the dispossession. Human nature does not reverse itself for our convenience. Men accustomed all their days to a most rigid system of caste could not be expected to hail rapturously the idea of paying court to bricklayers and brakemen.

It is equally true, on the other hand, that the coexistence of monarchy and democracy in the same country was always hard to explain to the Russian mind and many a Russian, otherwise well disposed, could never adjust himself to what seemed to him an anomaly or a contradiction in the plea that the Allies were the world's democracies fighting against the monarchical principle.[10] Then, too, some expressions made inadvertently and unofficially on the Allies' side were, in the diplomatic phrase, exceedingly unfortunate, and furnished the German propaganda with material it carried to the very ends of Russia. Nor was the situation helped by persons that doubtless with the best intentions held the time ripe and choice to lecture the Russians on the advantages of older and more conservative systems of government, particularly when they coupled these efforts with somewhat overfrank outgivings that the Russian experiment was sure to fail. Almost any people at such a time would be likely to assume that a wish fathered such a thought. King was a hateful word in a Russian's ears but with all his heart and mind he worshiped his Revolution.

And here was the next great point on which the Allies' cause went to wreck in Russia. I can conceive of no reason why we should not now deal frankly with what happened. It was greater history making, in those critical months in Russia, than had hung upon any battle of the war since the great days of The Marne. We are entitled to know the facts about it. Nothing could have been worse for the Allies' cause than the general failure of the western mind to grasp the sacredness of the Revolution. If there had been nothing else, I solemnly aver this alone would have been enough to drive the Allied ship upon the rocks. To the average, typical Russian his Revolution was the greatest thing that had ever happened in this world; he was sure of it, he could not see how there was the slightest question about it. I suspect that the verdict of the future will lean more to his opinion than to that of his present day critics, but that is not the point now; I am dealing here with history, not prophecy. He saw in the Russian Rev-

---

[10] He is referring to the fact that Britain was a monarchy as well as a democracy.

olution far more than the fall of the greatest and vilest autocracy of all modern times; he saw the beginning of the social regeneration of mankind. He saw a wonderful New Day at hand for the toiling sons of men, and the Russian Revolution bringing in the dawn. The very name of it was dear to him, dearer than his life, dearer even than his children. To speak slightingly of the Revolution was in his ears blasphemy; anything that threatened it touched the very nerve center of all the resentment in his nature.[11]

I suppose all this was naturally hard for an outsider of other environments and habits of thought to cope with; you could hardly expect old, formal diplomacy to understand such a situation. But the Germans understood it perfectly and played upon it with exceeding skill and success. And while they played, some part of the Allied citizenship at home and abroad leaned over their shoulders and kindly assisted by picking out the best keys. German agents, always starting with the basic declaration that the Russian Revolution was the grandest thing in the history of the world, pictured the governments of the Allies as "imperialistic," "capitalistic," "reactionary," "oppressive," and all animated by deadly hatred of the Revolution. The masses of the people in each of the Allied countries were represented as utterly opposed to the war but forced into it by their capitalistic rulers. In all these countries, and in Germany likewise, the proletariat, fired by the magnificent example of the Russian people, was about to rise, overturn the existing imperialistic and oppressive government, proclaim universal brotherhood and bring the war to an end. All that was necessary was that Russia, turning a deaf ear to the evil suggestions of the war makers, should hold steadfast to her way wherein she was the leader, bearing light to all the world.

If anybody objected that meantime Germany was an autocracy the answer was ready. All the Allied governments were as imperialistic as the government of Germany. Each was carrying on the war for selfish purposes of aggrandizement; each was a land thief. Great Britain was in the war only to seize the German colonies; France only to get Alsace and Lorraine; Italy only to get Trieste and Trentino. When this argument was backed around to the United States the difficulty of making it cohere might seem great, but not to these agile minds. The United States had gone into the war to extend its trade and for no other purpose. Besides, the United States was as imperialistic as any of the others, for look at its monstrous oppression of Puerto Rico, Cuba and the Philippines. There was a strange story I found to be in common circulation and belief that the United States had conquered Cuba, wresting it from its inhabitants and holding it now in hateful subjection. This concoction was made all the more vicious by the citation of an alleged American authority, a recent visitor to Russia. Yes, the United States was as imperialistic as the rest and much more capitalistic; for in the United States the workers were all slaves and dared not open their

---

[11] In this paragraph he catches the initial popular attitude about the revolution in a way many foreign writers did not.

mouths to complain. Yet, even in the United States, the revolt of the masses was close at hand.[12]

Chapters from the history of labor troubles in America furnished valuable material for appeals of this kind; the cases, sometimes true and sometimes fabricated, of men shot down by strikebreakers or convicted of crimes they had never committed. But there were other things cited quite as pungent of which much less was ever reported in this country. These were American pacifist or disloyal utterances against the war, and their effect was to bolster the assertion that the American people did not support their government and were about to rise against it.

As they never heard any denial of these assertions and never had any reason to doubt them, a large part of the Russian people became convinced that the American government was as imperialistic as Germany and that the name of republic, under which it sailed, was in fact, as so many of these orators asserted, nothing but a disguise for what was to all intents and purposes a monarchy. "America is no republic," said two hundred German agents turned loose upon the Field of Mars of a Sunday afternoon.[13] "It is a monarchy ruled by thirty kings and these kings are its great financiers and leaders of big business. They drove the country into this war for the sake of bigger business, fatter contracts and more profits."

There was a ready soil for the sowing of such seed and plenty of help for the crafty husbandmen that sowed it. The Russians had heard long before and often about the great capitalists of America, their power and cunning, and were in a mood to respond to any statement that these were among the worst products of the social system that for the good and freedom of mankind must be changed. Also, a horde of naturalized Americans and alleged Americans that were in reality anarchists, German agents, or professional trouble-makers, started for Russia the instant the success of the Revolution was safely achieved and added themselves and their propaganda of lies to the difficulties of the situation. Many of these had as their exclusive vocation the discrediting of the American Mission; some, indeed, after the Mission's appointment, had sailed in advance of it for the sole purpose of frustrating its efforts; and pretending to speak with authority as Americans they were able to work an amount of mischief out of all proportion to anything except their viciousness and impudence.[14]

---

[12] Here he is getting into one of the major questions of the day: America's territorial holdings overseas and how that made it easy for people to characteriz the US as just another imperialist country.

[13] He has slid into an exaggeration of German activity. This place was a popular site for many, diverse speakers.

[14] There were many leftist Russians under tsarism who had fled to the United States and were headed back home to Russia to help shape the revolution. Many were radicals and some were anarchists.

I ought not to overlook the fact, either, that some Russians of the extreme Left, which is to say the most radical element, had a belief that republics were worse enemies of any radical social advance than any monarchies could be. They reasoned that where workingmen had long been endowed with the ballot they became conservative and well disposed toward existing conditions, whereas under an autocracy there was always a chance of a proletarian Revolution that would have momentum enough not merely to abolish the political monarchy but the entire system of society as at present constituted. Such men taught diligently that the "bourgeois republics" of France and the United States were really the greatest obstacles to their own particular variety of the New Day.[15] If they were ever put to the test about such doctrines it was common for them to repeat the bald assertion that industrial democracy was easily possible without political democracy and much more important. Men of this order were at first few and of small influence, but they had an always larger following as the situation drifted on and they contributed nothing to the popularity of the United States.

Under these conditions, Russia, all the time weary of war, began to slip visibly away from the Allies. When they awoke to this fact the things they did to keep her were at first worse than useless. I do not know how I can better illustrate their total and fatal misunderstanding of Russia than by reciting this one little chapter of the melancholy story.

The government of the vanished Tsar had made a treaty whereby Russia bound itself to Great Britain and France to fight the war out to the end and not to make a separate peace. This treaty was now urged upon the Russian people as a reason why they should continue to fight. "You are bound by treaty, you know" (so ran the arguments that from the champions of the Allies I have heard and read hundreds of times); "you are our Ally and you must therefore go on with us." At first the Russians laughed; they were slow to believe that anyone could make that point in earnest. When they perceived that it was soberly urged they began at once to resent it.

For the simple fact was that, having repudiated the Tsar and all his works, they had not the slightest notion of being bound by any of his treaties. To their minds he had been a usurper, ruling without a vestige of right or authority; therefore nothing that he did, or said, or agreed to, meant anything or could mean anything to the Russian people, for he had never the least mandate from them to be their executive. They had no more sanctioned him or his government than they had sanctioned a government on the other hemisphere; he had no more right to rule Russia than he had to rule America; his treaties meant no more to the Russians than they meant to the Siamese. The Russia of today was not in any possible sense an inheritor, successor or assignee of the Russia of the Tsar. It was an entirely different Russia, new born

---

[15] Here he is speaking of the anarchist movement that flourished in Russia after the February Revolution, especially in Petrograd.

and born free. "Tell us nothing about the Tsar's alliances," men said. "All that is the blown dust of antiquity. Russia has opened an entirely new set of books."[16]

This view, although to anyone that really accepts the people as the one source of governmental authority it will seem reasonable and logical, some of the Allies never understood. Their failure to grasp it was a crushing defeat. It is not too much to say that the whole cause of the Allies pivoted on a sympathetic knowledge of New Russia and this point was the vital expression of such knowledge. The more, with a fatuous and lamentable blindness, they urged the treaties and the obligation of honor to fulfil them the worse they made the situation. That they raised the point at all was enough for many a thoughtful Russian, at first well-disposed toward the Allied Cause. It proved to him that the Allies did not sympathize with the Revolution and did not wish it to succeed. Otherwise how could they pretend for a moment that an autocratic government could mortgage the actions of the democracy that had overthrown it?

All this time there was another style of appeal that would have been effective, and the Allies never seemed to think of it. Wise men like Plekhanov and Kropotkin continually urged it, but nobody heeded them.[17] It was to point out and insist upon the fact (which was to be demonstrated to all when too late) that Germany was the deadly foe of the Revolution; that until she had been defeated no man need hope for democracy anywhere; that so long as she was powerful and under arms the life of the new-born Russian democracy was in peril.

If from the beginning the Russians had been convinced of this there would have been no Brest Litovsk negotiations and no breaking of the Russian line.[18]

There was another great key fact in the situation, so plain it stood forth like a great rock in a desert land and yet was strangely ignored by those to whom it should have been most significant. It was that here for the first time in human history had been erected a working class government. Whatever show there might be at certain times and in certain places of soft white hands, the only hands that actually moved any of the levers of government were hands rough with toil and fresh from the plow

---

[16] He is here dealing with a complex issue. Russia's continuing commitment to its alliances dominated much of political thought and debate in 1917. The initial Provisional Government was deeply devoted to it, and the rest of the 1917 governments found it essential also, although there was growing popular discontent of the continued war and the alliances. The Bolsheviks, after the October Revolution, looking for a way out of the war, soon turned to a separate peace after it became obvious that the Allies would not join in general peace negotiations.

[17] G. V. Plekhanov was one of the founders of Russian Marxism, but in 1917 he stood well to the pro-war right of almost all socialist leaders. Petr Kropotkin was a famous aristocratic anarchist who contributed to the early revolutionary movements, but by 1917 had little influence and died shortly after. Both men were famous internationally and to foreign visitors, but had little influence in 1917 Russia.

[18] Brest-Litovsk was the border city where Germany and the Russians negotiated what turned out to be the peace treaty of March 3, 1918.

handle. The Tsar was gone; in his place the peasantry was crowned absolute ruler of Russia. It seemed strange to me then and seems stranger now in retrospect that so many men whose business was to pluck out the very heart of existing fact irrespective of prejudice were able to blind themselves to this most important fact of all. The fate of the whole Allied cause might lie in the hands of Russia; the decision of Russia lay exclusively with its toilers. Whether men liked it or disliked it, this was the truth. Men might as well have thought of bringing their personal prejudices to bear against the physical fact, of a glacier. These toilers might seem rude and uncultured persons; they might be led of strange dreams; they might indeed be "lured astray by the pernicious theories of the Bolsheviks"; they might be "mad fanatics," "crazy Utopians" or deserve any or all of the other pleasing names so wisely bestowed upon them by some of the American editors. Nevertheless, Russia controlled the situation for the Allies and these men controlled Russia. If there were nothing involved but ordinary prudence it would seem well to acknowledge the facts of their position.

But so strong are the fixed habits of men's minds that in spite of these actualities, as plain as day to any observation, most of the Allied representatives clung resolutely to the fiction that the government of Russia must be like the government of other countries. They continued to assume, for instance, that in Russia men of wealth or rank or learning or business eminence or moldy political distinction or social fame or recognized standing in the world of the elect must surely be important factors in the existing situation. Such men were a power everywhere else, so assuredly they must be a power here. It is the literal truth that all of such men together had less influence than a single teamster from the streets of Petrograd or a towlsed-headed farmer from the Caucasus. That a man had money or had been prominent in finance or a leader in the best circles, instead of being any recommendation for him, was become reason enough why he should be now of the least esteem. The entire element that elsewhere is considered admirable and influential was here thrown into the discard; the useful had become the honorable in deed and in truth, and to an extent previous users of that phrase had hardly dreamed of. That a man should be listened to, it was necessary that he should be of the workers or have so proved his allegiance to the workers' cause that there was not a fleck of doubt upon his record. Even Intellectuals like Miliukov[19] that had long stood forth as political reformers and in the old days had gone to prison for their radical faith were now found to lag too far in the rearward of the procession

---

[19] P. N. Miliukov was the leader of the Kadet (Constitutional Democratic) party, the main liberal party, that had emerged after the Duma was founded in 1906 after the Revolution of 1905. Most foreigners and many Russians expected it to dominate the Provisional Government, with Miliukov as its leader. He took the position of foreign affairs minister in the first cabinet, but was ousted from that position after the April Crisis, where he had pushed hard to keep Russia's alliance and the foreign territory promised to it at the end of the war. He was well known to foreign dignitaries in 1917. Ironically, a historian by profession, he had actually lectured at American universities during a period when he had been forced to depart imperial Russia.

for anyone to hear them. It was the voice of the proletariat and the proletariat alone that was heeded.

Whether all this was good or bad is not the point here. The point is that the Allies never grasped the primary fact of the situation and so brought their disaster on their own heads. There seemed to be no way to make it clear in most of the Allied capitals that here was an entirely new experiment in human government and it must be handled in an entirely new way. The methods and precedents of traditional diplomacy were doubtless very precious but it happened that they would not work in this instance. No one need wonder that gentlemen steeped all their lives in the solemn ponderosities, stilted verbiage and elaborate red tape of an international intercourse buttressed by the ages should be unable to conceive of a state of society in which all this would excite merely savage ridicule. It is to be assumed that none of the statesmen of Europe were blameworthy for not seeing a change so startling, but the fact that they did not was none the less calamitous. If they had been wise enough to leave things alone the results might not have been so wholly disastrous, but the truth is they not only ignored the great change but they persisted in proceeding as if the old regime were still in full swing. A party of these formal diplomats with their long black coats, silk hats and air of portentous and inhuman gravity would have been glaringly out of place in the crowd of flannel-shirted and hard-handed farmers and blacksmiths that were now in charge of the government, but not so incongruous as the ideas of graveyard diplomacy that the old style statesmen would have represented. These are the facts in the case. Whether they were to be liked or disliked made again no difference. They existed; the situation demanded that they should be recognized; they were not recognized and the natural results followed.

There was another place where most of the statesmanship went wrong and that was in its unalterable attitude toward what was called the cabinet. In spite of all the evidence to the contrary, many eminent minds always insisted upon regarding this figure-head and marionette institution as the government of Russia. It was no more the government of Russia than was the table around which it sat. Much ado was made about changes in this ministry, whether to have this man as Minister of Finance and that man as Minister of Railroads were well or ill, when these changes were of little more importance than the dismissal of one stenographer and the hiring of another. Finally, the greatest stress was laid upon the selection of a prime minister [minister president], or president of the cabinet, and nothing could more plainly show the total misunderstanding of the Russian situation. For contrary to the universal belief in the United States, no prime minister of Russia, from the day of the Revolution to the fall of the First Republic, at least, had the slightest chance of being Russia's Napoleon, Moses, dictator or savior. Not one of them had any more real power over the destinies of Russia than any other good, competent, industrious department administrator might have.

All the time that most citizens of the Allied countries were looking for light and leading to a collection of excellent and worthy bureau chiefs, the real government of Russia went on almost without the world's notice. The real government of Russia was centered in the National Soviet, or National Council.[20] Here was the real power, absolute, final, indisputable; of the will of the Soviet the cabinet of ministers was the visible expression and instrument, simply this and nothing more; and so long as the Soviet was in existence or could be summoned or elected there was no more chance that any man could make himself the dictator of Russia than that he could control the tides of the sea.

The original title of the Soviet (in English) was the All-Russia Congress of Worker's and Soldiers' Deputies. It consisted of 830 delegates elected by universal suffrage from every part of the Russian dominions.[21] Most of the delegates were peasants; most of any body so chosen in Russia would be peasants. To make the title more consistent it was amended after a time to be the All-Russia Soviet of Worker's, Soldiers' and Peasants' Deputies.[22] It governed Russia in somewhat the way that the House of Commons governs Great Britain at such times as the British parliament has not abdicated, except that the Russian cabinet was much more truly and directly under the control of the Soviet. Even in minor matters, about which ministers usually have a liberal choice of action, the members of the Russian cabinet felt unfree to deal without the Soviet's sanction.

An incident in the too brief stay of the American Mission illustrates the relations between the cabinet and the real masters of Russia. The work of the Mission naturally divided itself in accordance with the experiences or special aptitudes of the members. Two were in urgent need of certain detailed information of a statistical nature. They sought it of the Minister in whose department the matter properly belonged. Day

---

[20] He correctly defines "soviet" as meaning "council" in Russian. However, it was already taking on a universal usage in Russian politics to mean specific political institutions formed in 1917 and after, and goes down thus in most writing about the revolution. I have changed his usage throughout so that it matches most modern writing.

[21] Not quite right. The soviets represented a majority of the population, but not all of it, and were not "elected by universal suffrage." The delegates here represented soviets from around the country.

[22] He somewhat confuses here and throughout the Petrograd Soviet and the first All-Russia Congress of Soviets and its executive committee. The Petrograd Soviet emerged out of the February Revolution and played a role in what he is describing, and its leaders soon organized the Congress of Soviets. They remained the real power all the way to the October Revolution. This was a little unclear to many visitors at the time, especially after the Bolsheviks took over leadership of the Petrograd Soviet in September and put it in opposition to both the government (still headed by Kerensky) and the moderate socialists, who still could claim Soviet leadership because of the first Congress of Soviets, even as their position was slipping. This sets the stage for the political turmoil of the October Revolution at the second All-Russia Congress of Soviets, which the radicals dominated.

after day passed but there came from that department nothing more serviceable than promises. On Monday the information would be ready at 10 o'clock Tuesday; at 10 o'clock Tuesday it would be ready that afternoon at 4; that afternoon at 4 it would be ready the next morning at 11. Nearly two weeks slipped by with no other result than this. One night the member of the Mission that attended the All-Russia Soviet put the whole story before the Soviet's Committee on Finance; the committee on the spot adopted an order to the Minister to produce the matter desired at 2 o'clock the next day or be summoned before the Council at 8, and at 2 o'clock the information desired was produced.

I cite this incident to show the nature of the real power that not only directed the ministry but controlled the destiny of Russia.

But if the Soviet seemed of little moment to the Allies, it was far otherwise with the Germans. German agents swarmed around the Cadetsky Corpus where the meetings were held; German agents were even members of the Soviet congress itself and put forth covert but effective efforts to help the German cause.[23] From the beginning Germany had made a far better survey of the situation than the Allies had made, for Germany perceived at once in whose hands the decision would lie and wasted no time on cabinets, ministers, nor long-coated diplomats. Von Bernstorff in Washington amazed all observers by his unerring perception of the fact that in the United States the one agency important to convince was the masses of the people. Similarly in Russia, the German agents took the full measure of the new propulsive force and adjusted themselves to it. They understood well enough that the inspiration of the Russian leaders was chiefly an altruistic vision of universal brotherhood, good will and cooperation, and upon this they played incessantly. They pointed to a world drenched in blood and tears, a world weary of war, and then to Russia as leading mankind to peace, sanity, friendship and the new social system. To anyone that saw what was going on behind the curtain the contrast between these tactics and the arguments of some of the Allies' representatives concerning the sacredness of the Tsar's treaties was most disturbing. While the Germans were using the very best appeal the Allies were using the worst.

From the first it had been so with the German maneuvers; it was so now in the marvelously adroit ways by which German agents continued to misrepresent to the newspaper readers of the world the true aspects of the Russian status.[24] In the hands of such cunning, able and unscrupulous manipulators the patriotic but unsuspecting

---

[23] He is quite wrong on this. Like many Allied government officials and visitors, he enormously overestimates German influence. He would have heard this constantly as an explanation for why things were going the way they were. Remember, he had just arrived when the "July Days" happened, and with it the enormous (false) charges that Lenin and the Bolsheviks were German agents.

[24] Again, like much of this section, he overstates what were popular ideas about German influence.

American press was tricked with a duplex system of rascality that might have fooled the elect. Stories were manufactured and sent over here to show that in Russia was nothing but chaos, anarchy, and devastation; only maniacs were listened to, only raving was their object. When the American press had properly denounced such conditions its criticisms were gathered, translated into Russian and widely circulated among the Russian people to convince them that it was really true, as they had been so often told, that America was the foe of the Revolution. Under the existing conditions I do not know of any ready-made machinery that would have met this devilish contrivance. Yet I cannot help remarking that often I had reason to wish the editors of my native land had a larger sense of the geographical aspects of humor. Doubtless it was very funny to write in the United States sarcastic paragraphs about the Bolsheviks and the ignorant Russian, but there was very little fun in standing on the Field of Mars and hearing that paragraph read to a crowd of indignant Russians.

The net result of all the German machinations was that they overwhelmed the Allies on a field never wisely nor efficiently contested. It was true enough that Russia was sick of the war and had every reason to be. Nothing like the slaughter of Russian troops had ever been known; the old Russian government had thrown away the lives of men like so much rubbish. Up to the Revolution the Russian casualties had been more than 7,000,000, in shambles we seem prone to forget if we ever knew of them. But it was also true that given anything to fight for the Russian was still one of the best fighters in the world. The great fact was always being overlooked that in the war up to the Revolution he had nothing to fight for. By a government he detested he had been ordered forth to risk his life in a cause he knew nothing about. He obeyed because he had on the whole less reason to fear the enemy in front than his tyrannical government at home, but there was always bitter resentment in his heart; dull, unformulated, vague, maybe, but still a hatred for the bloody work in hand and a feeling that it was nothing in which he had any interest. At last he had rid himself of the monstrous government that had thus imposed upon him a purely arbitrary power. The war into which that power had forced him had been to him a nightmare of senseless horrors; there was mourning in almost every household because of it; all for the Tsar, all for this hideous system of wrong, the mere memory of which filled him with loathing and rage. And he was asked now to continue to fight, to shed his blood and to postpone the New Day so dear in his dreams, all for the sake of a quarrel of this hated Tsar that he had harried forth! Why was it any quarrel of Russia's, the new Russia, free now from every other taint of this accursed Tsarism? Why should the Tsar's war, the worst of all his works, be still fastened upon the Russia that had thrown off all the other evils inherited from the same polluted source? And above all, why should a quarrel of the Tsar's keep the proletariat of Russia from being friends with the proletariats of other countries, their brethren and natural allies?

This is the way he felt, and however he may be open otherwise to criticism I admit that I have not been able to find a flaw in his reasoning, so far as it went. But there was always the one great point he never reached that would have changed altogether his convictions as to the necessity of fighting; he never sensed Germany's relation to democracy. And to bring that point home to him almost no effort was made. For the Revolution the Russian would fight to the last drop of his blood; for a quarrel of the Tsar's he cared not a straw, and would not care; yet the customary appeal to him was that he should fight in a quarrel of the Tsar's and not to preserve the Revolution.[25]

For months the question in the mind of every Allied citizen was whether Russia would continue to fight or would throw down her arms. For the reasons outlined here she elected to throw down her arms. I assume that what is wanted now is the truth about this historic situation. Here, then, is the truth, however unpalatable.

---

[25] In fact, both the Provisional Government and the Petrograd Soviet had worked, reasonably successfully, to convince Russian soldiers of the need to fight to defend Russia. However, when they decided on an offensive in June 1917, that disastrous event undercut the soldiers' willingness to fight.

Chapter II
The Real Propulsion and the Real Hope

For weeks after the Revolution of February, 1917, published views about Russia were so diverse and the news despatches were so often contradictory that a general impression in this country was of hopeless confusion. People often thought of Russia as of a vast, dimly lighted stage whereon they knew a drama was being enacted of overwhelming importance to the world but where all the actors seemed to be running about inconsequentially in a maze without plan or meaning.

Yet the keys to the play were, after all, simple and made of familiar elements of human progress, modified (as always happens) by temperament, institutions and ideals.

There is a place on the Trans-Siberian Railroad called Passing Point Number 37, a small brown speck on the illimitable emptiness of the Siberian plains. On the 10th of May, 1917, there came marching up to it a procession of farmers—about forty of them, I think—carrying red flags. They tramped solemnly along what in Siberia, by a violence of speech, is called a road, and is in fact not otherwise than a trail of ruts in black gumbo mud.

A passenger-train was coming from the east, from Vladivostok. At Passing Point Number 37 it took the sidetrack to wait for the train it was to meet. According to Russian railroad practice (which you might think a precept of religion punctiliously observed) the operation of getting these two trains past each other was to consume one half-hour, liberally inundated with swift and cheerful conversation.

Some of the passengers got out and swelled the verbal freshets. They talked with the ambulatory peasants; the peasants responded with joyous alacrity and no impediments of utterance that one could notice. It was after the Revolution; therefore more than two men could talk together in public without being prodded by a superactive gendarmerie; and a stranger might have thought that springs of speech, frozen for three hundred years in Russian breasts, had burst forth into grateful and tireless fountains.

Of a sudden the processionists were seen to line up in front of the baggage-car, to fall upon their knees there, to lift their hands in attitudes of prayer, the while they uttered strange, wailing cries and many wept.

What were they crying about? They had learned that in the baggage-car were the ashes of a Russian Revolutionist, an old-time hero of the long, long struggle. He had been condemned by the Tsar to one of the worst prisons of coldest Siberia; he had managed to escape and in the end to get to America. There he died, and his body was cremated. Now his ashes in a draped memorial urn were being carried in state back to that free Russia he had dreamed of and suffered for. But note: of the peasants that fell on their knees before that handful of dust that day, about one-half could not read. All of them, you might think, lived in a region literally farther from the world and its affairs than is Cape Nome or the Dry Tortugas. Yet all of them knew well enough the name of this dead hero and all his deeds, and instinctively all knelt before his ashes that they might testify at once to their reverence for him and the fervor of their own Revolutionary faith.

After which there were speeches. To assert this of any assembly anywhere in new Russia, Russia of the unchained tongue and the suddenly released soul, was in those days almost superfluous. Let there be a meeting of any kind and speeches came as infallibly as the tea and much oftener.[1]

But what did that procession mean, wandering red-flagged along the black ruts of lonely Siberia? It meant that the peasants were making a "demonstration." Demonstration about what? Demonstration against the sentence of death that the Austrian government had about that time secured against Frederick Adler, the assassin of the Austrian prime minister![2]

And that is Russia. I offer you herewith the keys to the play.

Because you find in this one little incident these things, perfectly typical, truly fundamental:

The Russian temperament and character, emotional, sympathetic, altruistic, generous, and quite indifferent to conventionalities:

The passion for "demonstrating," the tremendous impulse to let go with the feelings brutally suppressed so long by the monarchy now dead and gone, thank God for his infinite mercies:

The passion for oratory:

The warm, naive and somewhat dreamy feeling for the universal brotherhood and the sense of a world-wide cause.

That there was anything incongruous about a demonstration in Russia by Russians against Austria's execution of the death penalty upon an Austrian in Austria at a time when Russia and Austria were at war would never occur to them. Are not the workers of Russia, Austria, and all other countries brothers? Is not a wrong done

---

[1] Very true. Newspapers of the time, and visitors, commented on the many public gatherings, often spontaneous, and the wide range of speakers and subjects. A new word, *mitingovat* ("to meeting"), came into use.

[2] This is odd, because Siberian peasants normally would not have known of Adler. Apparently, some educated political exile was in the region. Victor Adler was an Austrian-Swiss radical known for the assassination of Austrian Minister President von Sturgkh in 1916. Ironically, he later became a major figure in European politics.

to a member of the proletariat in Austria the affair of members of the proletariat everywhere? Assuredly, comrades. Then let us demonstrate—even in remote Siberia, where nobody will ever know anything about it.

Also, you may see in this incident how deep in the heart of every peasant and toiler were the rudiments at least of the Revolution's creed, how widespread a fair understanding of the Revolution's history and meaning—spread even to the uttermost parts of the prodigious country, spread when there were no modern means of communication, before there were public schools, when there was no right of assembly, no free press and very little reading, and yet, for a marvel, spread competently.

In the light of this manifestation it seemed that even the most timid doubter might take heart of grace and be reassured that whatever else might happen, granted only that no outside power was allowed to break in, the old order was gone forever from Russia. If the people in this remote region had so great a fire for liberty and so clear a knowledge of it, the black blight of the Tsar would never come back. The tides of democracy might ebb and flow, there might be strange confusions and bitter struggles, but the Russian people having tasted freedom would remain free to the end. They might rule themselves well or they might rule themselves ill, but henceforth they alone would rule.

Yet it was, philosophically considered, little wonder that the world, sitting at such an unprecedented play, blinked and was doubtful. There was one day the imposing great structure of the most powerful autocracy on earth, centuries old, rockrooted, imperial and irresistible, cloud-compelling and remorseless. At a touch it crumbled together like the unsubstantial figment of a dream; vanishing without a trace, as if it had never been. Intricate, great systems of government, of police, of spies, of punishments, erected with long care and skill to keep the people down, all, all dried up and blown away like a mist, and behold these same subjugated people instantly and easily taking seats in a new machine, untried, just from the shops, and handling the controlling levers—with aplomb and for a time, at least, with a considerable show of success.

No wonder, I say, some spectators gasped and were puzzled. To the rigid, rectangular English mind, to the American mind that tries hard to be like the English, all this was not in nature. It was so different from Chelmsford Abbey, England, and St. Johnsbury in Vermont, that it must surely be bad. After all, and truth to tell, faith in the popular intelligence is not much of an Anglo-Saxon trait. What there is of such intelligence, we think, must be the product of long education, of training and of reading—much reading. But here was a country where only a few years ago 80 per cent of the population could not read at all; where the few newspapers were frankly corrupted and fiercely censored by the monarchy. Yet out of all this, lo, a people, by our narrow creed called unenlightened, who not only had a fine sense of liberty but being entrusted with the machinery of democratic government displayed an extraordinary avidity for its problems.

Plain, every-day working people, farmers right from the plow, laborers from the factories, producers and toilers, the "base mechanicals" of Elizabeth's famous sneer, the "common workingmen" of our own beautiful snobbery. The nobles, the wealthy, the middle class, the Intelligentsia, the propertied, the financial geniuses, the merchant princes, the employers here practically eliminated from public affairs. The Man with the Hoe had come literally into his own at last.

I dwell on this fact because it had potent and far-reaching effects. We may as well admit that this was one of the reasons why many persons in the Allied countries did not like the change in Russia and were at no pains to hide their discontent. I think with pride on the fact that there was less of this feeling in America than in some other quarters, but even here was no lack of persons that found the idea of literal and uncompromising democracy highly indigestible.

Nevertheless, that was the essence of the situation in Russia—democracy stripped down to its plainest terms and accepted unflinchingly. For in Russia the conditions familiar in other countries that have political freedom and the ballot box had been turned the other way about. In Russia Labor did not take orders; it gave them. For here Labor, being in an absolute majority, had assumed command, and nobody else had a word to say about the running of the machine. The bare, astonishing fact stood before the world that the country was being governed by about such peasants as marched through the mud to Passing Station Number 37 in Siberia and animated by about such impulses as caused them to demonstrate against the killing of a man in Austria and to fall on their knees before the ashes of a Revolutionist.

All this under the red flag![3]

Perhaps it was the color of that flag that most distressed the Americans and Englishmen that found themselves so completely out of sympathy with these upturnings. With us the red flag had always signified detestable anarchy, violence, blood, riot and ruin. In Russia it was now flying everywhere and under it moved a people that manifestly had no taste for any of the horrors of which the red flag was supposed to be the symptom, but loved peace and order. From Vladivostok to the Baltic and from Turkestan to the Arctic Circle, the simple red flag, without device, was the only flag to be seen. It had become the national ensign of Russia, superseding all others. In some of the Allied countries—shall I say our own?—the innovation caused perplexity and even pain. It was desired to keep flying the flags of the Allies, but in some states of the Union the mere hoisting of a red flag had been made a statutory offense and nearly everywhere else the sight of it was calculated to cause shudders in many a well regulated household. Yet there was the undeniable fact that officially the plain and unadorned flag of red alone could signify Russia. In some quarters the difficulty was avoided, not very deftly, one may think, by flying the flag of the old Russian mer-

---

[3] The red flag had a long history as a symbol of revolution, and in 1917 quickly became the symbol of the revolution and of authority within it; the Communists took it as the flag of their state.

chantman, red, blue and white, although this was no more nearly accurate than the flag of Sweden would be, or the flag of Argentina.

Yet the red flag, as flown by the new Russian democracy, had none of the horrifying suggestions that timid souls here would give to it. Contrary to the general belief, it did not mean anarchy, arson, barratry [official fraud], treason, stratagems or spoils. There was all the time I was in Petrograd a group of Anarchists making desperate efforts to cling to the skirts of passing events and as often as might be shift into the spot light. They used to parade whenever they could, and carry always with them their flag, and I take pleasure in relieving the anxious cares of the timid by saying that the anarchists' flag was black and not red. The meaning of the red flag, as adopted by the new Russian democracy, was universal brotherhood, simply that and nothing more. All the blood in all the veins of all the world is of just one even color. However men may differ in feature or in habits, the blood in their veins is always of the same tint, and this sign of the universal bond the Revolutionists had long ago chosen as the expression of their world-wide hope.

And in spite of the prejudice against it, I think not many Americans could have seen it in some of the places where it was flying without a sense of exaltation and an impulse to give thanks. Because, among the places in Petrograd where it was conspicuous was the great Winter Palace, once the largest, most imposing, most gorgeous and most costly royal residence in Europe. For almost two centuries there had flown from that flagstaff nothing but imperial ensigns that meant hatred, slavery, the iron fist and the rule it imposed upon subjugated millions. Thank God for the change!

Moreover, there were recent and poignant reasons for rejoicing. Those windows under the red flag of the new democracy had looked down upon Bloody Sunday.[4] In the square upon which the palace faces that sickening tragedy was played. They came there from all parts of Petrograd that morning, two hundred thousand men, women and children, starving, and fell on their knees in the snow and lifted up their hands and prayed to the Tsar, comfortable in that palace, for bread. The world ought not to forget the answer to their prayer. On the roofs of the great red palace, on the roofs of the War Building across the square, in the clump of trees on the south the machine guns were posted. And thence at a signal they began playing into the solid masses of people, playing streams of bullets as with a length of hose one might play water. And five thousand men, women and children fell dead where they were and thousands of others were wounded, so that the whole square was blotched and slopped with blood when all was over, and even the Tsar looking from his windows the next day was

---

[4] He is talking here about "Bloody Sunday," which inaugurated the Revolution of 1905, but he calls it Bloody Monday. Why he does so is unclear. Perhaps somebody in Russia used that term and he adopted it, or perhaps his usage is because it was familiar to Americans because of a "Bloody Monday" event that happened in Louisville, Kentucky, in 1855. What follows in this long paragraph reflects popular beliefs of the time. There was major killing, but less than he suggests, and Nicholas II was not in the Winter Palace.

nauseated at the sight.[5] And now the imperial ensign of force, wrong and murder that waved over the scene was gone forever and in its place was a flag that had been raised for the sake of an idea or dream of universal brotherhood and good will. It would be a strange order of mind that would not rejoice at the change!

At least to those that loved freedom, every symbol of it seemed good. In the old days of hatred and wrong troops used often to march through that square headed by a regimental band playing a hymn the refrain of which was "God Save the Tsar." And now the same band marched through the same square playing the new national anthem. And what was that? Merely the "Marsellaise," once proscribed in Russia and now become the universal melody.

On Sunday, July 1 [June 18, Russian dating], 300,000 people paraded in the square with band after band that played nothing else; all day the strains of that Revolutionary anthem echoed through the suites where Tsars used to sit and condemn to the living death of Siberia men that had said a few words in favor of human liberty. Three hundred thousand free men and women tramped to that tune over the stones that in 1905 had been drenched in the people's blood. Much was being made at that time of the excesses of the new democratic rule; much has been made of them ever since. I think that upon reflection it will be found that the simple fact of that one day's procession and the comparisons it enforced outweighed all the excesses of the Revolution, imaginary and real.

For if there was here a new experiment in government to make the timorous uneasy no one could deny that it was democracy's unescapable logic. After all, these people had no more than accepted democracy at par value. What they understood by democracy was direct government by the people, the great majority of whom were the toilers on the farms and in the factories; no "checks and balances," no artificial barriers to defeat the popular will and ensure government by property; exact political equality for all, universal suffrage, women at last freed from the surviving disabilities of the jungle, men freed from the political relics of feudalism. At one leap democracy had gone far beyond all its previous achievements. A new country had been launched with new ideals and new purposes and the world must rub its eyes and awake to the new birth.

It will always, I suppose, be an open question whether pure snobbery was not the chief factor in the unreadiness many of us showed to recognize the essentials of the new order in Russia. The subtle and deadly influence of Germany and the lack of any organized effort to combat her methods, achieved the defeat of the first Russian Republic, but certainly it was no prevision of any such fate that misled us into the strange notion so common at that time that we had some divine call to teach democracy to those well-meaning but deluded creatures.

---

[5] The number killed and seriously wounded on Bloody Sunday was probably about 1,000, in several places in St. Petersburg, plus many more during the disturbances of the next year.

THE REAL PROPULSION AND THE REAL HOPE 27

I may say with confidence that no one that visited the Cadetsky Corpus in the days when the All-Russia Congress of Soviets met there entertained any such thought.[6] Sitting in that famous place nothing could well seem more absurd than the suggestion of instructing in democracy persons that went so surely and swiftly to its actual practice.

The Cadetsky Corpus was the old name of the West Point of Russia, the training school for army officers. It covers an astonishingly great area on the side of the Neva opposite to the Winter Palace beyond which lies the business center of Petrograd. There is a large number of white stone buildings, none of more than two stories, and much campus between. It was in the great hall of this school, a place of mark in Russian history, that the All-Russia Congress of Soviets of Workers', Soldiers' and Peasants' Deputies held its sessions, and as this body, being elected, must have been a fair expression of the will and mind of the Russian people it was and is surely worth study.

The whole country had been divided into districts on the basis of the population, so many people to a district. Each district had chosen one deputy, all adult men and women (except lunatics and criminals) being endowed with the franchise. Consequently, there was not in the world a more truly representative body nor one with a mandate better based upon the orthodoxies of democracy.[7]

The principal entrance was upon a side street leading away from the river. It was wholly unpretending and the only indicators of the present occupation of the building were the crowd that hung about, and a small sign in red on white cloth displayed on the wooden steps. The crowd, I remember noticing, was composed only of working people. Workers likewise were the soldiers outside and in, and all of them privates. I never saw in the building, I think, any soldier higher than a corporal except one deputy that was a captain. But he was likewise a peasant and his rank was of Revolutionary origin, so that he was no true exception. Entrance was by ticket, but tickets were very easily obtained, and the part of the hall set apart for the public was invariably

---

[6] He now begins to describe the first All-Russia Congress of Soviets, a meeting of representatives from city soviets and other organizations from around the country, June 3–5 (16–18). It was an effort by the Petrograd Soviet leaders to formally transform their authority from just Petrograd to the entire country. It set up a Central Executive Committee, which in fact was made up especially of the leaders of the Petrograd Soviet, and distinctions between the two were vague at the time. Only in September, when the Bolsheviks took control of the Petrograd Soviet, did the two organizations find themselves at odds. The "Bolshevik Revolution" came when the Bolsheviks emerged from local elections in control of the Second All-Russia Congress of Soviets in late October (November by the Western calendar, and hence the terms "October Revolution" and "November Revolution" coexist for the same event).

[7] This is not quite accurate. The soviets of this time in general represented most of the population, directly or indirectly, but some were excluded, especially the old upper and middle classes. Even for the workers and peasants and soldiers it claimed to represent, that was done somewhat erratically. Nonetheless, it was more an "elected representation of the people" than any other institution, including the Provisional Government.

crowded no matter at what hour the sitting might be. At the top of a short flight of steps from the street I turned to the right and traversed two very long, bare corridors, where at intervals appeared a citizen soldier on guard with his bayonet on his rifle, the Russian custom. On one side of these corridors was the drill ground and parade ground of the cadets and on the other, through windows in the wall, I saw a great apartment filled with iron cot beds. I asked what these were for and was told they were the beds of the delegates. To save time as well as money they had requisitioned the cots of the cadets and camped on the spot. In the adjoining building I was shown a cellar, equally great, filled with the crudest of wooden tables and wooden benches. This was the dining room of the delegates. They saved time and saved money likewise by getting their meals on the spot. The repasts, I can testify, were of the most primitive character—sausage, black bread and tea.

The Congress was an industrious body; it frequently began its sessions at 11 o'clock of one morning and did not adjourn until 3 o'clock of the next. It had assembled strictly to do business and the deputies found little time for anything else.

The great hall of the cadets, in which the sessions were held, occupied an upper floor of the building in which I had found the refectory. It struck me as remarkable that the lower hall and to a considerable extent the stairways were filled with bookstalls where young women were busily engaged in selling literature, and still more remarkable that all of the literature they sold was of an advanced order of economic or sociological philosophy. I took pains to examine the wares offered and found nothing more ephemeral than Kautsky and Lassalle.[8] There were eighteen stalls at which these mental stimulants could be had and I am obliged to say that all seemed to be doing a good business.

The Cadets' hall was not well adapted to the purposes of an assembly, being of such extraordinary length that persons at the rear could with difficulty make out even what was shouted at the other end and seemed to be looking down a vista of oppressive length upon human puppets on a remote stage at the other end. Once these walls were adorned with the portraits of dead Tsars and the flags of Imperial Russia. All were vanished now; ripped down with joyous acclaim on the day of the Revolution. In their place appeared everywhere the red flag as the only decoration; except on the wall at the entrance end, where one could read this startling motto, done in white upon red banners:

"Workers of the World, Unite! You Have Nothing to Lose but Our Chains!"

Many a time in America we have heard this call proclaimed from the disregarded soap box or have read it carelessly in the literature of agitation. Few of us expected to meet it emblazoned on the walls of a national legislative assembly that

---

[8] Ferdinand Lassalle was a prominent early nineteenth century political activist and initiator of national-style social democracy in Germany. Karl Kautsky was a prominent German socialist of the time who criticized the Bolshevik seizure of power.

was very likely determining the fate of the world. Karl Marx would seem to have been vindicated at last.

The rear one-third of the hall was reserved for the public. Delegates occupied the rest, seated at the transported old desks of the recent cadets. On the high red-flagged platform at the extreme end sat the guests of the Soviet and its officers, including that redoubtable Chkheidze, the chairman, of whom the world was to hear farther. At his left was the rostrum, a plain reading-desk for the speakers.

To sit up there and look out upon that historic gathering was to see the whole Russian situation plotted like a map in the clearest colors before you. It was also to gain a new and peculiar sense of the power that lies in the mere mentality of determined men. There they sat, representing all of the organized force of Russia, holding its destiny absolutely in their hands. At their will ministries resigned, administrations rose or fell, armies advanced or retreated, the future state of millions was determined. And but five months back and not one of these men had so much as dreamed that he should see Russia free. Then most of them were bowed patiently and hopelessly under an autocratic and medieval government that they hated; many were in exile because they had dared to oppose that government and never expected again to be free. And now, they sat there and moved their ruler about the country like a poor little pawn on a chess board and cut up his property for the benefit of the nation.

I think it safe to say that this was the most extraordinary legislative body that had ever met anywhere in this world. It surpassed even the National Assembly of Revolutionary France, for that was after all a middle-class affair; advocates like Robespierre, journalists like Desmoulins. If we come to democratic assemblies of later days, American Congresses and legislatures are all lawyers; British are chiefly land-owners and the sacred white fatted calves of the ancient families. But this national legislature of Russia, as I have before pointed out, was composed of persons that worked with their hands or those so closely allied with labor that their essential interests were with the workers. It might consistently have advertised, "No lawyers need apply." Also, no business men, employers, captains of industry or members of the better classes, for none of these had great representation in its membership. If then, as the world has generally believed, only the legal mind or the scholastic mind is truly fitted to conduct a legislature, the attempt of these new and incongruous elements to make laws and transact business should have been not much better than ludicrous.[9]

Many persons in America, when they heard of the rise and functions of the All-Russia Congress of Soviets, speculated much about the Duma, which had generally been accepted as the real Russian parliament and was fairly well known to be composed of safe, sane and conspicuous citizens. It was hard to surrender this famous body, wrung from the slow hand of the Tsar and hailed everywhere as marking the

---

[9] While he correctly describes the innovative character a political assembly of such a broad and lower class nature, he tends to leave out that the leaders, whatever their radicalism, were primarily intelligentsia of the old educated classes, and thus of somewhat higher social origin.

dawn of representative government in Russia; yet the fact was that the Duma was no more. Pride of the American press and hope of conservatives generally, it breathed its last even while I was in Petrograd and I was privileged to attend the obsequies. They were characteristically and beautifully Russian. The Duma had been a body chosen by the landowners and a few other fortunate persons. It never represented Russia; it had no relations to the Russian people. It was, of course, in an autocracy better than nothing, for while only a few had the right to vote for it, still it was voted for. But when the Revolution came and swept away the entire machinery of antique absolutism there was no longer any excuse for a Duma. All the people, in free election, were now choosing their own legislative body. Still the Duma continued to meet and debate, as if it had yet a function, or possibly from force of habit, history does not tell us which. One day in the question came up whether this relic of a bygone age had not better be abolished since it was no longer of the slightest use to anyone; but to my surprise the proposal met with bitter opposition.

"This is a free country," delegates argued. "Any assembly ought to be allowed to meet as much as it pleases and discuss anything that suits its fancy. But since the Duma is no longer the national legislature we are in favor of cutting off all its salaries and all its expense list." Which is exactly what was done—with the utmost gravity. Whereupon they bore out the corpse of the Duma and buried it. If the Russians are shy of a sense of humor anywhere it is in regard to their public affairs.[10]

It was common for first time visitors to the Congress to be much impressed with the large number of soldiers' uniforms in the delegates' seats, the seemly well-fitting olive green tunic that makes a British army coat look like something cut out with an ax; the belt, the high black boots; even in the breathless hot days of July, the high black boots. Seeing the overplus of these uniforms visitors usually swept to the conclusion that the Congress was a military body. This was an error. Military service in Russia was universal and compulsory. The uniformed men were not only soldiers; they were farmers, factory workers, day-laborers, carpenters, stonemasons, who had been called to the colors and were wearing the uniform of the service when they were elected to the Congress as workers and by workers.

Few foreigners in Petrograd had any knowledge of the Congress or paid attention to it, notwithstanding the fact that it alone had real power in Russia. Aside from four of the newspaper correspondents I could not find a foreigner that had ever been inside the hall. There was a strange mistake common among them that the Congress represented only Petrograd and vicinity. This blunder, which was inexcusable, arose from the fact that there were two entirely distinct bodies having somewhat similar names,

---

[10] The Duma, originally created as a relatively democratic assembly out of the Revolution of 1905, was remade in 1907 as a relatively unrepresentative assembly. Its leaders played a role in the February Revolution and the creation of the new political regime, but its unrepresentative nature led to its quickly becoming irrelevant, and its term of existence officially ended October 6 (19).

the All-Russia Congress of Soviets of Workers', Soldiers' and Peasants' Deputies and the Petrograd Soviet of Soldiers' and Workers' Deputies. The Petrograd Soviet consisted of about two thousand members created at the time of the Revolution by the Petrograd garrison to look after the soldiers' interests. It was without mandate from the people or power over any public affairs, but it was continually confused with the Congress of Soviets.[11] As the Petrograd Soviet used to amuse itself daily by passing some such resolutions as that there should be no more private property in anything or that sunflower seeds should be free to all soldiers, this confusion did a great deal of mischief. The German propaganda, of course, seized upon it instantly and used to deluge the American press with news of the apparently insane transactions of the "Workers' and Soldiers' Soviet," always creating the impression that this referred to the Soviet and was of some national significance. Whereas in fact it had somewhat less relation to the national action of Russia than resolutions by the New York Board of Aldermen would have to the national action of the United States. Long after the All-Russia Congress of Soviets had adjourned this adroit malpractice continued. I have no doubt it contributed materially to the American misunderstanding of the Russian problem.

So far from the All-Russia Congress of Soviets being in any way a local body, it represented every part of Russia, even far-away Asiatic Russia. Only thirty of the 830 delegates came from the Petrograd district. Among the rest were fishermen from the Lena River, swarthy cattle-men from the Crimea, and everything between.

Five of the delegates were women. I have often wondered why the triumph of universal suffrage in Russia received so little attention elsewhere. The world seems to have elected to dwell forever on the natural confusion that attended the overthrow of the old system and to ignore the evidences of an enlightened and progressive spirit that were really far more important than all the petty disorders. So far as we in America were concerned, certainly, the fact seemed to cast some doubt upon the sincerity of some of our democratic inclinations.

The moment the wormy structure of imperialism fell there was but one thought in the mind of everybody, and that was universal adult suffrage. Nobody opposed it; everybody was for it—instinctively. There may have been reactionaries in Russia that were impressed with the arguments against woman suffrage so common in this country, but I never heard of them. I never heard any Russian say that woman's place was the home and her interest the wash tub. I never heard one of them complain about the degrading influence of the ballot or speak with bated breath of the terrors

---

[11] He mistakes the roles of the two soviets. The Petrograd Soviet was formed during the February Revolution by workers and soldiers and quickly became the de facto center of power. Its leaders later organized the national Congress of Soviets and dominated it also. The Central Executive Committee, created at the congress, was dominated by the same Menshevik-SR leaders of the Petrograd Soviet, but provided a place for "national" leadership. The Petrograd assembly and leaders remained the main force.

of the ignorant vote. Faith in these discoveries seems now to be limited to our own land of the free.

In some other respects, also, our record when compared with that of the lowly Russians seems not quite all that we might desire. After fifty years of ceaseless campaigning we won in America full suffrage for women in nine States and part suffrage for women in three or four others. After sixty years of argument and five years of what was really civil war, the English suffragists won to a part of the justice they demanded. In Russia, suffrage for women was achieved in a moment and without discussion. It was taken as a matter of course. To the Russian mind democracy meant democracy; it did not mean an unjust arrangement under which one-half of the population was denied any share in the government that governed them.[12]

I should think that contemplation of these facts by self-righteous British and American critics might tend to jar somewhat the belief in a supernal call to teach democracy to Russia. Also, they might be thought to counterbalance to some extent a failure to keep a treaty that the Russian people never made and never recognized.

The truth is that democracy in Russia was neither a dream nor a jest but to all reflective Russians a thing of the utmost seriousness. In the many years they had struggled for it without the least assurance that they should ever see it, they had learned to look upon it with a respect probably impossible to people that come by it through the easy route of inheritance. Despotism had taught them the value of freedom, and being now free they seemed resolved to have democracy in all their affairs and to keep it.

One day while I was in Petrograd the Yacht Club received applications for membership from two women. I hardly have need to say that in the old days such a thing, if conceivable at all, would have caused strong hearts to faint and police spies to discover new candidates for Siberia's cold wilds. But now the point was raised at once that since the Revolution men and women in Russia were upon a level of exact equality, and that automatically women had become eligible for any organization that admitted men. The point was held to be well and truly taken and the women were voted in.

There is in America general conviction that the people of Russia are totally inexperienced in the practice of democracy and of course must therefore fail in their first use of it. A few days after the Yacht Club incident Petrograd afforded the judicious an unequaled chance to see whether this notion had any substance. There was an election for a new City Congress. As in the elections for the Congress of Soviets, the suffrage was universal; about hundreds of thousands of people used the ballot box

---

[12] A major debate arose immediately after the February Revolution over giving women the right to vote, crossing political partly lines. Women quickly organized large demonstrations for the right to vote—on March 19, the League for Women's Equal Rights mounted an enormous popular demonstration in Petrograd. On July 20, the Provisional Government gave women universal and equal political rights. Russia was the only major country to have those at that time. Note, however, how few he says were in this assembly.

for only the second time in their lives. I had an opportunity to observe the function closely. It moved like clock-work; one would have thought these people had been voting all their lives. There was a registration list, a committee composed of soldiers, workingmen and householders to manage the polling-places and scrutinize the voter's right; there was no disorder, no confusion, no discoverable chance for fraud. Some things were done better than we ever did them. The polling-place was invariably some public building; no basement poolroom or pickle-shop. Frequently it was on the ground floor of a former Grand Duke's palace, put at last to a reasonable use. There was no electioneering, there was no crowd of Red Leary's Toughs.[13] Women went in and voted with ease, dignity, and, methought, a quiet but ineffable satisfaction. Seven different tickets were in the field. Each voter was provided at his house with a copy of each ticket, duly certified. The end of the ticket was perforated. At the ballot-box the voter was checked upon the registry list, the perforated end of his folded ticket was torn off, officially stamped and spiked, and he put the rest into the box.

There were cast in the city 722,000 votes; total population a little more than 2,200,000. Of the 722,000 all but about 140,000 were cast for the candidates of parties that proposed the most sweeping changes in the whole social structure and the downfall of the last remaining castle of the old order. The bourgeoisie had practically disappeared.

Similarly the proletarian flavor of everything about All-Russia Congress of Soviets was unmistakable. Not only were its members workingmen and workingwomen but so were its spectators. As a rule there were not more than six other persons in the hall besides myself that wore linen shirts and white collars and these six were among the correspondents and reporters that occupied the space on the floor to the right and left of the raised platform. To look over the vast assembly of serious, intent faces that crowded the long room, row after row to the exit at the rear, was, I believe, to see the real Russia, and I never found any other one spot that equaled it for compendious observation. I have in my time known thousands of audiences but audiences of this kind were new to me. There they sat hour after hour, drinking in every word that fell from any speaker, silent lest they should lose a syllable. Those at a distance made ear trumpets of rolled-up newspapers; they were intolerant of the least movement or noise that caused them to lose any precious crumb of the proceedings. It was as I told you in the foregoing chapter—here was the proletariat of Russia, hands upon the levers. No man could despise them now; with a breath they blew ministers in or out. In the hall, where long lines of gorgeous dead Tsars used to look down from the walls, and gorgeous living Tsars used to watch the military training of gracious youths of the governing class, and all things seemed comfortably settled forever, plowmen and teamsters sat to debate whether Nicholas Romanoff, late of the Gorgeous Ones, now

---

[13] John "Red" Leary was a famous American bank robber and tough who was killed in a fight in 1874.

a prisoner of state, should be allowed to vote like other plain, common citizens. Wonderful was the change, brethren! Few, I think, that deliberated upon it were ready to believe that a people so started upon the self-governing road could for any long time be tricked away from it.

On the floor the delegates were ranged from left to right according to their politics; which means, according to the intensity of their Revolutionary fervor. This arrangement, of mysterious origin, is common in continental legislatures. The Left means men of radical conviction and the farther to the left you go the more radical they become. In the Russian All-Russia Congress of Soviets the man that sat next to the window on that side was so hot a radical he seemed to be about to break out into flames. From his tropic neighborhood moving to the Right the temperature steadily diminished. In the Center sat the men who while devoted to the radical cause were not beyond the habit of reasoning about it. Next to them on the Right began the men reckoned as conservatives. After a time it struck me as a remarkable fact that the most extreme conservative on the Right, a man, let us say, that by most of his colleagues was regarded with suspicion and as not quite fit to go down to drink tea with, was a man that in the United States before the war would have been looked upon as a dangerous and incendiary character and one that the reactionary press would have blacklisted with joy.[14]

The Left in the All-Russia Congress of Soviets believed that the Revolution had hardly begun and that before it should end every existing landmark of a social system they abhorred would be swept from sight. The Right believed that the Revolution was a splendid and worthy thing but its work was done and Russia should now think only of building a new structure on the ruins of the old. Between the extreme Left and the extreme Right was the real driving force of the Congress, the men that wanted the Revolution to sweep on and do many more things that ought to be done, but were unwilling to see it misuse and lose what it had already gained.

Left and Right, perhaps I should explain to those unfamiliar with European assemblies, mean looking from the platform; it is the chairman's left or right.

The group on the extreme Left in my time was composed of the famous Bolsheviks with Lenin as their leader. Much as I saw and heard of him, I was never able to arrive at a satisfactory conclusion about him except as to his extraordinary ability. Any desired shade of opinion of him could be had, ranging from hero and martyr to devil, but none seemed on investigation to have any sure basis. I once had in my possession copies of the documents that seemed to prove he was in the employ of Germany, the same documents with which a newspaper of Paris afterward sought to drive him from public life, and as these were stolen from me by the German spy that broke open my trunk on my way home I can only suppose that by the Germans at

---

[14] Remember that he is describing an institution that was almost all socialist, with a small number of other leftists.

least they were regarded as important. On the other hand many of Lenin's bitterest opponents in Russia, with these documents before them, declared that the man was absolutely honest, however mistaken, and the papers that seemed to implicate him were forgeries and slanders. Indeed, it ought to be remarked that they never have been validated and for the most part would be inadmissible evidence in a court of law.[15]

One thing about the man that could not be denied was his extraordinary magnetic power over a certain order of mind; if he had been able to make in the same way a larger appeal, or had appeared at a different epoch, there is no telling where his power might have stopped. Among his followers was a certain small group that looked upon him with almost superstitious reverence. With sincerity they regarded him as a superman sent to lead the world from its war bondage, and no evidence against him, no matter how supported, would have had weight with these. Yet there was always to my mind something elusive about him; even in his oratory he had never the fine, frank, outspoken fervor of Tsereteli or Kerensky, but neither Tsereteli nor Kerensky had such a devoted following.[16]

There was never anything elusive about Trotsky. He was an open book and one to most minds extremely attractive. I have never seen a better type of the fanatic; he believed without the least question that the Bolshevik theory was about to triumph in the world to the world's salvation. He had warm and splendid visions of the whole human race united in bonds of enduring friendship, while the working class in each country conducted what little government should be necessary. His mental engine seemed never at rest but toiled even when it traveled but in circles; he was generous, kindly, believed he hated all capitalists and capitalistic governments and could no more see a second move after he had conceived a first than he could fly to Mars.

The Bolsheviks were not numerically strong in the Congress, but made an unreasonable noise for their numbers. On one of their test proposals, while I was there, they secured 144 votes, but their regular strength was estimated at 119. They were not at that time a political party but merely a faction of a party.[17] Parties in Russia had a

---

[15] This section on Lenin and the Bolsheviks is very good, one of the best written by a foreign visitor at the time. He correctly understood that the popular charge that he was a German agent was wrong. The latter idea had widespread popularity because the Germans had helped Lenin (and other radicals) return to Russia. One can still find it in some writings today.

[16] Kerensky and Tsereteli were two of most important political figures of that time—Kerensky as a member and then head of the Provisional Government, Tsereteli as perhaps the most powerful figure of the Petrograd Soviet for the first several months of the revolution.

[17] The terminology of parties was confusing at the time, although he gets them pretty well. The Bolsheviks were not quite officially a separate party rather than a wing of the Social Democrats, but were in fact, and soon were in name as well. Socialist Revolutionaries were an agrarian oriented party, and the largest in Russia, but in 1917 became divided into at least three factions, including what he calls the Maximalists and Minimalists. The Mensheviks and

more formal organization and method than anything we are familiar with and were as the sands of the sea for number. I could never pretend to fathom all the differences among them and never met anyone else that could. Doubtless there were such persons but they must have been of an abundant leisure. I knew that in most cases the differences were very slight: beyond that, the waters of knowledge began to shoal rapidly for me. Among the important parties there was first the Social Democratic, then the Social Revolutionist, then the People's Socialist, then the People's Liberty, then the Cadet or Constitutional Democratic Party, and then the others. The two great parties of the country were the Social Democratic and the Social Revolutionist. So far as the finite mind could learn they had practically identical creeds. I was never enlightened as to what they had to fight about, but anyway it was of no importance, for the real fight was not between but within them, after this fashion:

The Social Democratic Party was split between its Bolsheviks and its Mensheviks. The Social Revolutionist Party was split between its Maximalists and Minimalists. Bolsheviks and Maximalists were the same; Mensheviks and Minimalists were the same. The quarrel was between the Bolsheviks-Maximalists on one side and Mensheviks-Minimalists on the other, and more than once threatened to rend the All-Russia Congress of Soviets asunder.

The substance of their disputes was one of the first great facts in the Russian situation and necessary to be well understood by anyone seeking the keys to the play.

The Bolsheviks-Maximalists were Syndicalists[18] and wanted the Government to take over all the factories, banks, land and utilities—at once.

The Mensheviks-Minimalists wanted the Government to take over all the factories, banks, land and utilities, but not at once; because they did not believe the time to be propitious. Practically, that was all except for the matter of dreams and visions, previously spoken of. The Bolshevik-Maximalist group dwelt in an imaginary world wherein they saw the present social system rolled together as a great scroll and a new one of vague but gorgeous construction let down from heaven to the sound of celestial minstrelsy, themselves constituting the *deus ex machina*. The Menshevik-Minimalist group usually succeeded in keeping their feet upon the ground and their projections out of dreamland. I may as well concede that the extreme Left of the Bolshevik-Maximalist group were Anarchists,[19] although they would never say so, nor train

---

the SR main faction, its center, worked as allies in 1917, while the Bolsheviks and Left Socialist Revolutionaries often cooperated, and did so immediately after the October Revolution especially.

[18] Not quite accurate, although a popular idea of the times. Syndicalism was a particularly radical movement globally.

[19] The anarchists were emphatically not Bolsheviks nor Left SRs, although they were often listed together in the somewhat confused terminology of the times. In general, his descriptions of political groups, especially the socialists, are better than most American writers of the time.

with the little Anarchist element in the city. Not the clamorous and cheap vaudeville type of Anarchist that perennially plagued sober men by careering with mad yells and in automobiles about the city, but philosophical Anarchists, I mean. Syndicalism seems to be a kind of a poor relation of Anarchism, anyway, and often to be found sidling toward the Anarchist home.

On all the broad general principles of Socialism and democracy Bolsheviks-Maximalists and Mensheviks-Minimalists were agreed, and together they constituted about three-fourths of the Congress. You might say, indeed, that all the Congress and all Russia were saturated with Socialism and nearly everybody was a Socialist, the only difference being in degree and in ideas as to the practical application of theories. That being the case, the notion that was continually advanced in certain British and American quarters of taking by the hand these simple children of nature and leading them kindly up to the primary democratic principles of Thomas Jefferson and Lloyd George was to the judicious a joke that never lost its savor. Among these people Revolution had long passed beyond all such primitive processes and democracy meant industrial democracy as much as it meant the right to vote, and industrial democracy meant the division of the products of industry among those whose toil had created such products.[20]

In other words, it meant the practical elimination of dividends and interest and with this, it was hoped, there would be an end of want on one side and luxury on the other.

For some reason never well explained it was always extremely difficult to get in America any recognition of these facts.

But here comes in a question that seems to me the next great point on which the future of Russia hinges. How come so much of the mass of Russian people, viewed by all the truly learned as ignorant and stupid, to seize upon a social philosophy so new to the rest of the world and so far in advance of it? Because these wise men that have so liberally condemned Russia to a state of hopeless ignorance have not themselves progressed a foot outside of the Jeffersonian realm of thought; to this day they can see nothing but political democracy. Yet the inferior Russian, booted, vodka-soaked and all the rest, lays hold upon this new conception of a life without poverty and without superfluity, a theory not simple, not rudimentary, but advocated in many dusty tomes by ponderous thinkers practically unknown to our superior world. Here, it seems to me, is a wonder, both historic and suggestive. That in the old poisonous days of darkness and autocracy, when the gag was on every man's lip, the police-agent listening at every man's door, the Government watching every press, the chill fear of Siberia in every heart, illiteracy a paralyzing cloud over the whole land, there should still spread widely among the people, by stealth and mostly by word of mouth, such an economic and social creed—I must doubt if that achievement can be equaled, or approached,

---

[20] An important distinction most American readers would not have known.

in all the histories of men. Such being the case, I come to the greatest question of all: Where, then, shall we draw the probable limit to the potentialities of such a people? I mean, if they can do these things under the most difficult and discouraging conditions, what will they not be capable of with peace, universal education, and some part at least of that economic freedom of which they have had an alluring vision? And I believe, dwelling impartially upon the modern history of Russia, that it might have been possible to overlook and be tolerant of many features of the situation that for the time being were hard blows to the western nations, for the sake of the unimpaired capital of Russian character that still lay behind.

Still it was plain enough that their social philosophy and their very devotion to it made them and their country liable to defeat and destruction. Their dreamy fantasies about universal good will and brotherliness in a time of war opened the door to the German spies, agents, bribe-mongers, secret propagandists, and the crawling creatures that spread poison over the Field of Mars every Sunday afternoon, and the world had afterward bitter reason to lament that liberality.[21]

Second, it was, I suppose, inevitable, that having these spacious dreams of social betterment and the New Day the most active minds in Russia should get but a twisted notion about the war. It was the war that blocked their way to a world without poverty. Anything, therefore, that would end the war would be a blessing, and since, in the new dispensation, national boundaries are to be of no consequence, why hesitate to end the war on the geography of July 1, 1918, or of August 1, 1914, or upon any other? And if it were suggested to them that the surest and best way to end it was to put forth every effort to defeat Germany, this they rejected with scorn for the reason that they construed their altruistic creed to contain an injunction against all war and because under that creed, the German workers were their brothers and they must not go forth to fratricide.

Nothing could have better suited the German propaganda.

These influences were reflected day by day in the Congress of Soviets, where the precious moments went by and the unopposed Germans created for well-meaning deputies an imaginary America and an imaginary road to peace.[22] To the Congress itself, so different from legislative bodies of the Anglo-Saxon experience, the facile Germans easily adjusted themselves. I was sometimes tempted to believe that its wide difference from the House of Commons constituted the burden of its sin in British eyes; so easily those that have democracy come to believe their way is the only way of having it. Yet in its stern application to the work in hand, its tireless industry, in its rapid and competent handling of public affairs, any observer would have been obliged to admit this legislature needed no instruction from any other. Certainly there was

---

[21] The Field of Mars was a major gathering place for speakers of all kinds and views; those he describes as German agents would in fact have been Russian radicals.

[22] Again, his tendency to identify things as being created by German spies.

nothing about its proceedings that caused me to regret the American Senate. It was, by comparison, a very large body, and the accepted rule of human experience is the larger the body the smaller the chance to transact business. Taking together the voting and the merely fraternal members there were more than a thousand of them. I noticed particularly that while the proceedings were on none of the delegates slept, talked, read newspapers nor moved wearily about after the manner of our Congressmen and Senators. All of the Russian legislators were in the habit of sitting still and attending strictly to business. Perhaps one reason for this was that the speeches were always short. From all the information I could gain I judged that they were also full of pith and matter; I know that they were not allowed to wander from the point under discussion; I have too often known them to be brought back sharply to their course by Chkheidze, the chairman, to be under any misconceptions about that.

Chkheidze seemed to me one of the two most remarkable men in the Congress and the soviets. He was a Georgian and spoke Russian with a marked accent and not always perfectly. Yet his power over the assembly was extraordinary. He was a thin, hawk-faced man, with a short clipped, grizzled beard concealing most of his face; sharp, cold blue eyes, an aquiline nose, a powerful jaw, and quietly masterful manner. He was of about the average height but always looked much taller on the platform. He usually wore an olive green flannel tennis shirt with a rolling collar attached. When he walked he bent slightly forward and seemed to be able to walk without making any noise. He seemed under-vitalized, for his hands were always cold and his face bloodless, but if reports were true of him he could perform astonishing feats of endurance. In the weeks the All-Russia Congress of Soviets was in session it was said he hardly slept at all. He would preside over the Congress until it adjourned, which might be at 2 o'clock in the morning, and then hold conferences and receive visitors until a short time before the hour of reassembling, when he would disappear for a brief rest and be ready to go on duty again, guiding for hours without apparent fatigue a body by no means easy to discipline or command.

His success, however, was undeniable and often wonderful. He had manifestly a gift for such employment; he had been chairman of the Petrograd Soldiers' and Workers' Congress and had steered that turbulent body through a thousand storms. It seemed to me, watching him, that much of his success lay in an instinctive barometric sense of coming trouble. He presided not with a gavel but with a sharp-toned bell, and I could see him in advance of any disturbance quietly reaching his hand out for that unusual symbol of authority. The instant a clash seemed imminent he rang the bell and the danger point passed without an upheaval. It was his ceaseless vigilance, too, I believed, that kept the speakers on the track; his ready bell seemed to sound warning in advance of actual wanderings. I have seldom seen a more orderly body;

even in the hot days when the row precipitated by the Anarchists was uppermost and the Bolsheviks started to leave the hall, one could not really say there was disorder.[23]

The other man that impressed me was Tsereteli, at that time the Minister of Posts and Telegraphs—so-called, though any other designation would have done as well. In a land of orators he and Kerensky were the most famous and admired. Like Chkheidze, Tsereteli had been a victim of the Tsar's oppressive government; ten years he had spent in a frightful dungeon of Siberia. Like Chkheidze again he was ordinarily among the most reticent of men, a habit that had undoubtedly grown upon both in their prison experience. Tsereteli was tall, slender, with dark and rather sunken eyes and a singular manner of detachment, as if he were always thinking about something else than the subject in hand. He answered questions or responded to remarks with the utmost brevity; I never knew him to volunteer any conversation on his own account. He had at one time a great popularity and in the Bolshevik disturbances of July it was his powerful appeal that restored quiet. His oratory seemed to be spontaneous and unpremeditated. He began slowly and not always without some trace of hesitation and gradually rose to the full measure of his unusual powers. He had not so great a reputation as Kerensky, but I believe his was nevertheless the greater oratorical gift.

Kerensky struck me as in general intellectual power, also, not up to the stature of Tsereteli and Chkheidze, and in that judgment I believe thinking Russians will generally agree with me.[24] It is a remarkable fact and should be most instructive of the power of the press, that Kerensky's greatest reputation was in the United States. It was only here that he was hailed as a "dictator," man of the hour or ruler of the tempest. In the space of a few weeks the press of America created a hero, mapped out his work, and discharged him i[n] disgust when he failed to perform the task it had assigned and of which he had never heard.

For the simple truth is that M. Kerensky was never the "dictator" of Russia, was never clothed with any such power, never attempted to exert it and never was in any position to save or change the situation by means of any authority conferred upon or attainable by him. He was not only no dictator but probably never had any

---

[23] His description of the very important Chkheidze is excellent. It, plus the one of Tsereteli that follows, provides an unusually good description of two of the most influential men of the time. What he does not point out is that they both were Mensheviks—and, critically, leaders of the more moderate socialist bloc that led Russia from late March to September 1917—and continued to play a role later and through the civil war.

[24] Kerensky was a moderate SR/Trudovik and a key figure in consolidating the February Revolution and creation of the Provisional Government. The only socialist in the first cabinet of the Provisional Government (March and April), for many he symbolized the revolution. He became minister president (head of the Provisional Government) in July and held that until overthrown by the October Revolution. By that time his popularity had declined dramatically. Unlike Tsereteli and Chkheidze, he wrote numerous memoir accounts of the revolution, which helped confirm the belief that he was the most important person of the February–October period.

dream of being one and could not have been if he had desired. Because no man could be dictator of Russia without the consent of the Russian people and there were no people under the sun at that time so absolutely hostile to anything in the nature of a dictatorship as the Russians. All the time American newspapers were picturing M. Kerensky as about to perform this or that awe-compelling feat of leadership, that most excellent and well meaning man was without any power to do anything except as the Congress of Soviets might direct. But of course this was but another instance of a wish that fathered a thought, and those that hesitate to believe unreservedly in the people's power to rule themselves are driven irresistibly to the refuge of a Napoleon even when one has to be created for them out of the impossible materials afforded by the Russian situation.

The scorn with which the same newspapers treated their imaginary "dictator" when he seemingly failed was as irrational. No one, situated as he was, without real power and confronted with an inevitable event, could have done any better than he did. He was an administrative chief and in the details of his department did well so long as he lasted. But it was perfectly evident from the time he took office that some such crisis as the Bolshevik upheaval was certain unless Russia could be set right in its mind in regard to the Allies and their purposes; and when the crisis came it span out of its way not only Kerensky, who had no power, but the Congress of Soviets, which had much.

The stories about Kerensky's "dictatorship" were like the stories about his feeble health. According to the pathetic accounts that over here called forth sympathetic poems and endless laudation this poor man was already doomed to an early grave but dragged out his last few days that he might be Russia's Napoleon and lead her back from the perilous cliffs of radicalism to safer and saner paths; very likely of constitutional monarchy, for instance, or something else not too advanced for our susceptible nerves. While I was in Petrograd, at least, there was not the slightest indication of invalidism on Kerensky's part. He was attending with great energy and industry to his work as Minister of War, he was making frequent addresses of great power and eloquence, his step was as quick and firm, his voice as full and steady, his hand clasp as powerful and warm as if he were in perfect health. A robust man, certainly, he could never be. But there was not the slightest indication of extreme ill health.

I did see Tereshchenko,[25] the brilliant young man that was then Minister of Foreign Affairs, perform one night an act of conspicuous endurance, for suffering from an ailment that produces probably the most intense agony of which this mortal frame is capable, he stood and listened to two long speeches and made a long response and

---

[25] Tereshchenko, a very young non-party liberal, played an important role in 1917. He was the only person besides Kerensky to serve as government minister the full period from the February Revolution to the October Revolution. After Miliukov's resignation following the April Crisis, he moved from finance to foreign affairs. After the Bolsheviks took power, he moved to France and resumed his successful business career.

never allowed a suggestion of his suffering to appear in voice or face. Tereshchenko was thirty-six years old, an Oxford man, a great traveler and an able diplomat in the old school. It seemed a pity that a career that seemed so promising should be cut short on a mere prejudice. He was hated by the Bolsheviks because his father had been very rich. There was, however, no question about Tereshchenko's patriotism or that he had as much essential sympathy with the radical cause as any man could have that had been brought up at Oxford.

I spoke a moment ago about Russia as a land of orators. I used to marvel unceasingly, both at the Congress of Soviets and on the Field of Mars, at the very high order of this art that was offered. I remember in particular one night at the Congress when there appeared a typical example. A delegate came to the rostrum to speak on a question that affected the farmers, of whom he plainly was one. He had a round close-cropped head, a sunburned visage, and the big brown veinous hands of labor. He wore the soldier's tunic and high boots and looked as if he might but now have emerged from the trenches. After listening a little my interpreter told me the man was unlettered and probably illiterate. Among the delegates were twenty that could not read or write. Perhaps he was one of these.

Yet he spoke with an astonishing fluency, never hesitating for a word. He had all the resources most orators obtain by laborious study and effort. He knew how to produce effects. He modulated his voice to suit his thought, he dealt in sarcasm, made his hearers laugh or be serious, built in his climaxes. Now he started upon his peroration. Steadily he carried it along, up and up until he burst over his listeners a magnificent torrent of emotion and they were upon their feet, cheering.

Yet this triumph of the uttered word, which seemed so wonderful to me, did not seem to any Russian a thing phenomenal. The like had frequently been heard in the Congress of Soviets.

It is partly upon such revelations of reserve power that I based my confidence in Russia's future, partly upon the Russian character and partly upon some other things to be dealt with later. But as to the point of character, I beg leave to draw attention now to one suggestive fact.

The police system of Russia, in the old regime, was the most elaborate, extensive, complete and perfect police system ever devised. Of a sudden it was abolished—utterly, and without a remaining fragment, abolished. Nothing took its place, you might say. A few men in citizen's clothes volunteered as militia, a white band on the left arm as the only insignia of office, often without even a club as a weapon.

But without any police force, Petrograd, having more than 2,200,000 inhabitants, remained one of the most orderly and peaceful of cities, more orderly and peaceful than any great city in America.[26]

---

[26] An idea stated by many foreign visitors, probably reflecting both what they saw and what they were told. In fact, there was a steady growth of violence and crime.

THE REAL PROPULSION AND THE REAL HOPE

With such a capacity for self-discipline, self-restraint and a decent respect for the rights of others, the future of these people seemed hard to limit.

But the absolute requisite of their rise was, as President Wilson so plainly saw at the time, that they should have a chance to work out their own problems unhampered by foreign interference, and above all that the blight and curse of the Prussian theory of life should be kept from them. All the great peoples of the world have soared to their highest achievements from some period of national stress, danger or upheaval. It seemed safe to believe that, granted liberty and independence, from the dark, straining days of 1917 a free and democratic Russia would rise to dazzling heights to do things beyond the records of almost any other people.

Even in its days of bondage Russia had produced some of the world's greatest literature, greatest art, and greatest music.

Chapter III
Two Aspects of the New Faith

When, at the deep-toned signal of the Revolution, up blazed in Russia the essential but long suppressed democratic passion of the people, it seemed for a time as if all skies were warm with its reflection. It was like the sunburst of a new religion, broad enough to embrace all the children of men and lofty enough to satisfy their aspirations. That a light so promising should have been later darkened, even for a time, by the philosophy of force, is a sign of mourning in the history of human freedom and likely to be [such] unless we can bring ourselves to a long perspective and admit something of the uncertain twilight that has always marked the moving of the democratic spirit on the face of the deep.

But while all the serious aspects of the New Russia were at first sound and good I shall never deny that some of the surface manifestations were a trial to the nerves of persons late come from a more staid and conservative view of democracy.

In the middle of the night, somewhere near the heart of Siberia, I was projected from sleep by the voice of our assistant train manager, raised in vehement protest:

"*Niet, tovarisch, niet! Niet!*"

That is to say, "Comrade." After the Revolution everybody in Russia was "tovarisch"—the waiter at your restaurant, the surviving scions of a frayed and draggle-tailed nobility, colonels, captains, privates, everybody. To hear it in this instance signified nothing. The train manager might be talking to a trackwalker or to a fallen grand duke.

Immediately there arose a chorus of deep gutturals, evidently conveying dissent, and then, to a sound of sharp scuffling, the car rocked suggestively.

I thrust my head through the double hangings of silken stuff that adorned the air-tight window of the stateroom once sacred to the Tsar's eldest offspring. We were stopped at a station that stood apparently alone in a great moonlighted void, and about one hundred armed men, mostly with the ugly four-cornered bayonets sticking from their guns, were trying to climb the sides of our train. Their route was by way of the couplings, the buffers, a handy lantern bracket, and so to the roof.

The whole thing was excellently staged for a film play of a holdup by bandits, and all men knew that if bandits were needed, the Buriats,[1] close at hand, had an over-

---

[1] Buriats are a small Mongol population of the Lake Baikal region.

supply. But these actors were not of that industry. They were only regular Russian soldiers on their way home from the front.

The train manager now ran forward and made a few well-chosen remarks in vigorous native speech, whereupon they came clambering down. Once upon the ground, they explained that they meant no harm. But this was a free country now. The railroads belonged to the Government. The Government belonged to the people. They were the people. They wanted to ride. Then what was the matter with riding on their own railroad?

In those days such episodes had become familiar all about Russia and were usually quite innocent. We saw them every day. The logic of the soldiers might have some flaw in it, but evidently it was a flaw that bothered them little. Train after train met us or was passed by us, loaded with soldiers. Soldiers jammed the compartments, the aisles, the platforms, the steps, the couplers, the roofs; all moving homeward, happy, sunburnt, dirty, and harmless. They rode carefree and fare-free; a soldier's papers were the only ticket required. It was a free country. The Government hauled them without charge and lost thereby some profitable traffic, but in the existing conditions it was too wise to suggest another view of the matter.

The sheer rebound, all this was foreordained and not alarming, the rebound of a people that for centuries had gone heavily laden under a preposterous and half-mad tyranny. It might easily have been something worse. Sometimes, in fact, it took shapes that were only amusing or mildly irritant. When one of the American commissioners remonstrated with a Moscow taxicab skipper for perilously fast driving through crowded streets, this judicious person replied that the country was free now and if the passenger did not like to travel fast, he could alight and walk, at the same time drawing up to the sidewalk and opening the door to facilitate his exit. Restaurant waiters commonly preferred the pleasure of conversation to the duty of bringing your soup, and when a delay of perhaps forty minutes was brought to their attention (delicately, if you desired to complete your dinner) responded that the country was free and the son of freedom defied the tyrant, or words to that effect. A barber in a Petrograd shop, being petitioned not to cut too short the hair of one of his victims, observed that the country was free, and clipped it to the scalp.

In the matter of domestic service, householders entered upon diplomatic communication with servants leading up adroitly to the proposal that the floors should be swept or the dinner cooked. Old relations of employer and employed received some salutary and needed joltings; with the turn of a hand the principle was established that he that sells his labor for wages does not necessarily sell also his soul, and no one could deny that in itself beneficent was the discovery.

Soldiers rode free upon city street cars as upon the steam railroads, with the result that they soon had the Petrograd trolley lines practically to themselves. Nobody else could get in. To be sure, a man, if young and agile, might sometimes find an insecure footing upon a brake beam or an axle box, but I mean as a general rule.

Thousands of soldiers, having nothing else to do, rode up and down the line all day, eating sunflower seeds and enjoying the scenery,[2] with no other results than merely bringing the civilian population to unwanted exercise. The street railroads are owned by the municipality. Before the Revolution they used to make a net profit of about 9,000,000 rubles a year. After the Revolution they were operated at a loss.

It was with sarcastic reference to these conditions that the national convention of Cossacks, meeting at Petrograd in early July, adopted unanimously this minute: "That word be sent to our families at home that the Cossack soldier is true to his traditions. He neither rides on the trolley cars, chews sunflower seed, nor pursues women."

However, these were but incidents and not important. Whatever might be the surface excesses, underneath there was the strong feeling for democracy and a determination to have it. That this was sometimes bedeviled by evil agencies was plain enough even then and the process was accelerated later. I think the story of the Black Sea fleet, which came to a head while we were in Russia, is as good an illustration as I can cite and I like it for another reason, that it shows how much of the trouble that followed could have been averted by any apt efforts to meet the enemy with his own weapons.

Since the Revolution, the Black Sea fleet, headquarters at Sebastopol, had gone on well enough. The men were in full sympathy with the new order, in favor of continuing the fight, in favor of keeping discipline somewhere near par. They had, it is true, established a committee, or soviet elected by themselves, that conferred with the commanding officers and protected the interests of the sailors, but this was in fact well and not open to objection from any reasoning mind.

Kronstadt, the great naval arsenal of Russia, was a hotbed of a kind of dreamy philosophy, half natural Anarchism and half the diabolical work of German agents.[3] All things considered, there was not then a great deal of this weedy faith, but what there was produced a disproportionate crop of trouble. One day an emissary from Kronstadt appeared at Sebastopol and began to preach mutiny to the Black Sea men.

No doubt he was a master hand at this employment; no doubt he knew the Russian mind. He drew the usual entrancing pictures of a world without war, of the universal brotherhood, of the cooperative commonwealth, and then urged the sailors

---

[2] The reference to sunflower seeds here and elsewhere reflects that eating them was a popular activity of ordinary people. After the February Revolution and the end of police restrictions, soldiers eating them in the streets became common, as noted by some other commentators as well.

[3] NOT the work of German agents! Kronstadt, the huge naval base next to Petrograd, was a center of very radical leftism, especially in the July Days, and thus a prominent issue while he was there. Many liberals and others he talked with would have described them as German agents at that time, a time when anarchists and Bolsheviks were being falsely described as German agents.

to start on this road to happiness by disarming the officers, shooting all that might object, and declaring that they would fight no more. He won them, or most of them, to take his visions for real.

The committee, or soviet, for reasons of ancient experiences, had no love for the admiral in charge of the fleet and was glad of a chance to depose him. It now made haste to order that all officers should surrender their arms and it should be the supreme and only authority. Each ship had its own soviet, which sent delegates to the general soviet of the fleet.

The officers gave up their arms as requested, all except the old admiral. He said he had been many years in the navy, had never surrendered, and did not purpose to begin now. So he threw his sword and revolver into the sea.

This was the situation when Admiral Glennon of the American Mission[4] arrived on the scene. He had no knowledge of it until he found himself received by a committee of the sailors instead of by the officers he had expected. The sailors desired him to address them. So he spoke, through an interpreter, words of moderation, wisdom, and common sense, and when he did that he touched the potent spring in the Russian make-up. The typical Russian, with all his idealism, loves good sense and calm reason. Admiral Glennon showed that he had a warm heart as well as a wise head. He talked sympathetically, and when he had reasoned out the situation the soviet decided, all but unanimously, to rescind the former order and call the strike off. The arms were restored to the officers and peace to the fleet.

Old General Cassius M. Clay, who was minister to Russia just after the Civil War, used to insist that there was a strong psychological similarity between Russians and Americans and, excellent judge of men that he was, he had expert knowledge of both nations.[5] I think he was substantially right. Anyway, Russians get along better with Americans than with any other people, and on just grounds we may believe that if Americans could have had a fair chance to dispute the field with the German propagandists they would have defeated them before almost any Russian audience.

I have mentioned the Revolutionary ideals about industrial democracy. Some strange eddyings of the tidal wave were shown in this direction also, doubtless under more or less Teutonic instigation.[6] The men employed in many factories and some

---

[4] Rear Admiral James H. Glennon was sent as part of the Root Mission alongside Russell. This was one of the remarkable events of the time of the Root Mission in Russia.

[5] A prominent American general of the US Civil War era. A Kentucky planter and politician who opposed slavery and freed those he inherited. He helped protect Abraham Lincoln in the first days of the Civil War and then left for Russia as ambassador. The idea of a basic Russian-American similarity on some characteristics was a popular idea of the time.

[6] If one ignores his ongoing crediting or blaming events on German influence, he here begins a good description of the economic issues of the times and their impact on worker salaries and worker-management disputes. Prices were going up sharply during the time he was there, and along with it demands for salary increases and the resulting industrial tensions.

coal mines made demands on their employers that started icy chills along the spinal cord of Capital and thickened the gloom that dwelt about the Petrograd Bourse.

If they were getting two rubles a day, it was common for them to demand twelve. The gasping employers protested that it would be impossible to continue the business on such terms, in some cases pointing out that the increased wage account would be a greater sum than the total business of their enterprise. To this the men responded that the division of the products of industry had always been grossly unfair and the object of the Revolution was to right it. There were factories in Russia that had been returning annual profits of from 100 to 200 per cent and paying to their employees not more than enough to keep soul in body. All such conditions were now slipping off the edge of the roof, and if the proprietors did not care to divide fairly, they could close the shop and get them home, for the men would not work except on the terms proposed.

This was painful tuition to the proprietors. The old order had changed indeed. Where were now the handy black-coated police that used to put all labor disputes to the fine arbitrament of the saber and make quick work of them? Where are the snows of yesteryear? There was not a helping hand anywhere; no police, no militia, no armed guards.

"Take the factory, then, and run it yourselves," said more than one owner, perhaps making a gigantic bluff.

Sometimes the men called it; sometimes they threw out the proprietor or manager without waiting for such an invitation. I suppose the like could hardly happen anywhere outside of Russia, but the men actually began in many instances to operate the mills, and sometimes and for a while at least they operated them successfully. Those that wonder over this development will be those that have never heard of the achievements of the Russian cooperative societies. Of course the men oft-times failed and had to recall the proprietor or manager and compromise on what they could get. But the world may well take heed of the fact that sometimes they made the enterprise go and annexed unto themselves the profit.

I saw an iron foundry in Siberia where the erstwhile proprietor, dwelling in a handsome house close by, was privileged to see from his windows his former employees going to and from the works he had long commanded and from which he was now excluded. It is possible that if the ideas that ruled in July, 1917, had been allowed to work out their natural conclusions an amicable arrangement might have been made for these experiments. It is useless to imagine what might have been. The extremists overcame the reasoning men and all such hopeful chances seemed to go down together.

When the industrial disturbances were at their worst they had reduced the factory output to 40 per cent of normal. This was regarded as calamitous. The era of the extremist came and caused the 40 per cent to seem in retrospect almost good.

Fundamentally, the men that struck in the Russian factories had fair occasion. They had always been most wretchedly underpaid; even in the best of times they lived in horrible poverty; with the increased cost of living brought about by the war their choice was to better their condition or starve. The methods they chose were not in the handbook of etiquette, nor according to precedent and custom, but as a rule they brought home the bacon, or at least some of it, and the worst that they suggested was better than the flat ruin that fell upon the land thereafter.[7]

In the cases where the men took the factories and did not fail with them the fact was due, I suppose, in a way to exceptional circumstances, to the demand for a needed article or something of the kind; but primarily it was due to that strong capacity for united effort and solidarity to which I shall have many occasions to refer.

This reminds me again that the most important fact about the Russian situation seemed to be the fact hardest for Americans to understand. It was that as to all matters connected with the social state of man in the world, the average thought of Russia had gone in advance of the average thought in the United States.

When Catherine Breshkovskaya,[8] the beloved "Babushka" of the Russian Revolution, was in this country, our foremost sociologists made much of her, and among them she formed the acquaintance of a lady renowned for good deeds, and in some circles viewed as occupying the farthest outpost of social advance.

The next day the "Babushka" asked, in slightly frostbitten accents:

"Who is this lady, Miss —— ?"

She was told that Miss —— was a leader of thought and action, universally esteemed.

"Well, I can't see where she comes in," sniffed Mother Catherine, who had picked up some American colloquialisms. "I talked with her two hours last night and"—with great disdain—"she seemed to me nothing but a philanthropist!"

In the course of her visit she frequently expressed her astonishment and disappointment that the American reformers seemed never to have thought beyond the idea of being nice, charitable, and kind. They had no social vision and no suspicion of another state of society than the system of tooth and claw they saw around them. This usually awakened astonishment in Russian reformers; they felt they had outgrown the intellectual era of the United States.

No doubt it was equally true about political philosophy.

"Where," asked the leading American liberal newspaper in July, 1917, "where are the Thomas Jefferson democrats of Russia?"

---

[7] Throughout he, like most visitors, failed to note that Russia was undergoing rapid inflation; one month's adequate income was not adequate shortly afterwards.

[8] Ekaterina Breshko-Breshkovskaia, the Babushka—"Little Grandmother of the Russian Revolution," as she became known—was one of the founders of the socialist movements and the SR party, spent about four decades on and off in prison. She had traveled to the US earlier, and all 1917 American visitors focused on her. Upon her return to Petrograd in 1917 she was greeted as a great heroic figure, but by then her very moderate politics joined with her age to reduce her influence on events.

The question amounted to a jest. If anyone should take to Russia the political principles that we call Jeffersonian, they would be regarded precisely as men view the dug-up fossil bones of the dead geologic past. Thinkers would put on their spectacles and look the relics over and say: "And men really used to deem these things important? How odd! But they are a nice addition to our museum shelves."

The most tolerant Russian had a tendency to regard us as but little more enlightened than an English Liberal, and an English Liberal he viewed as a kind of political Hottentot.[9]

Sometimes the estimate was still more uncomplimentary. I happened to remark to one of the most intellectual women of Russia, a leader in the great Social Revolutionary party, which at the time of my visit was in a majority in the First All-Russia Congress of Soviets, that a great many persons in the United States knew and admired her work. "I do not care to be admired in the United States," she remarked icily.

"Why not?"

"Because the United States is a dreadful place, without progress and without hope."

"Where on earth did you get that impression? Some enemy hath done this. We are, as a matter of fact, a pretty good sort."

"No," said she, "I got it from studying your American literature. When I was in prison in Siberia they allowed us to read only one American publication, a magazine. I read it carefully every month for ten years, and I saw from the kind of matter it published the characteristics of life in your country. It is hard, cruel, selfish, uninspired, and given over to profit making, material aims, and business. In those ten years of reading I could never discover the slightest indication of progress, of social enlightenment, nor of any purpose to keep abreast with the world's thought. I came to have a horror of America. It must be one of the most backward countries on earth."

"What was this magazine that thus foully slandered the land of the free?"

She named one of our most famous periodicals esteemed as a triumph of culture and art.

Those that had felt the democratic fervor animating most Russians for months after the Revolution could never bring themselves to believe it could be permanently subjugated by the triumph of the extremists in October, 1917. When these with some battalions of armed men dispersed the constituent assembly and seized a government they had no mandate to operate,[10] the deed assaulted the strongest convictions of

---

[9] The American delegation, and the British and French ones of about the same time, were viewed by the Russian socialists (who, one must remember, already dominated Russian governments at all levels) to be behind the political, social, and economic times that Russia was headed into.

[10] He seems to jump from Bolsheviks seizing power in October to the Constituent Assembly in January 1917 without reference to the Second Congress of Soviets.

the majority of the Russian people. Why, then, did they submit to it? Because, in the first place, the Bolsheviks came with a fair pledge of peace for all the world and the Russians were sick of war. In the next place, the Bolsheviks had the Petrograd garrison and the great majority of the population of Petrograd. All the offices of the government were at Petrograd; nothing was easier than with these advantages to seize those offices and declare the new government. Third, there was the drawback of an undeniably widespread ignorance. And finally, the Russian temperament objected to meeting force with force, and expecting a general election to be close at hand preferred to wait for that, when they knew the Bolsheviks would be defeated and a government with a popular mandate take their place. There were some other reasons that might not appeal much to the western mind but were powerful upon the Russian make-up because they were of the nature of fatalism.

But while Russia waited, the Germans made their master stroke, outplayed the dreamer Trotsky, seized the Baltic provinces and threatened the new democracy with annihilation.

Nevertheless, to know so much of the Russian spirit as is contained in the deeds of the men and women that gave their lives or their liberty that Russia might be free is enough to banish pessimism about the future of these people; even in the face of the undemocratic achievements of the Bolsheviks, faith remains unshaken in all that know the records. No nation that could produce such martyrs and make such sacrifices will permanently surrender itself back to despotism. As, for instance, the case of Maria Spiridonova, which might be entitled The Story of All for One and One for All, and is the true epitome of Russia as in faith it is.[11]

In 1905, she was seventeen years old, a schoolteacher at Tambov, twenty-four hours by rail east of Petrograd. To look at her you would have said she should be going to school herself, she was so slight, girlish, and innocent. The governor of her province was the greatest official rogue and beast in Russia. This is saying much, for he had conspicuous and able rivalry for that distinction. But I think he was the worst.

This slender, quiet little maid, contemplating some choice performances in cruelty that the governor delighted in after the Revolution of 1905, said: "This fiend has forfeited his right to live, and if there is no man in the district that is man enough to kill him, I will kill him myself."

So she got a revolver and hid it in her muff, for the weather was cold, and went in the morning to the railway station where the governor was to take a train for Petrograd. She walked up and down the platform, as if she were waiting for a train, until he appeared and began in his turn to walk up and down the platform, attended by his suite. She waited until she got a clean sweep at short range, when she pulled out her revolver and shot him through the heart.

---

[11] Here he reverts back to talking about the Revolution of 1905 and other historic events while focusing on Spiridonova.

The wolves that then conducted the Russian Government concluded that they would make of her a memorable example. He that was lost had been a precious adornment of the old regime, skilled in cruelty, in upholding the sacred existing system, and in keeping the lowly in their appointed place. Besides, it was a period of unrest, and wise policy dictated that these cattle should be shown what happens to such as revolt.

So they inflicted upon her the most frightful tortures that even their depraved ingenuity could devise, and beyond that is nothing that can cause pain, physical and mental, for these were artists in that line that could have instructed (and astonished) the Apaches.[12] She weighed about ninety pounds, she was utterly helpless in their hands, and they tortured her not for one day but for many.

But observe, these things took place in a fortress, buried from the world and supposedly from human knowledge. In some way the news got abroad and the mutterings of the people began to assail even the dull ears of wolfdom. I suppose it was rather the moral force of millions of men united in one judgment than the least regard for anything they might do. Anyway, the wolves stopped the kind of torture they had been perpetrating on this girl and brought her to what they miscalled her trial. The original intention had been to put her to death when it should appear that she had been made to suffer enough. It was now determined that instead of killing her outright her executioners should send her to die by inches in a Siberian prison: solitary confinement for life. The prison selected was 500 miles from a railroad station, far north in a region almost inaccessible. There she was thrust into a cell underground and without natural light. Eleven years she passed in this dreadful place.

When the Revolution upset wolfdom and with it the Government that was guilty of this and ten thousand other such atrocities, an order was sent from Petrograd to release all political prisoners. The jailer refused to obey it. Some time elapsed, of course, before the fact reached Petrograd. Then an order was despatched giving him twenty-four hours in which to set his prisoners free, after which, if he still refused, he would be taken out and shot, a file of soldiers being sent along for that purpose. That there might be no chance for error or evasion, the new order gave the names of the eight women political prisoners that the records showed were confined in that prison, Maria Spiridonova being one of them. The jailer now summoned the eight into his presence, women rescued from the living tomb and restored to the daylight they had never expected to see again. Some thought it was a dream; some a new and more refined cruelty they were called upon to undergo. One was convinced she had died and the proceedings related to her soul and not her body.

The jailer told them they were free.

"Wait a moment," said Maria Spiridonova, "I see here only eight. There are two more women in this prison."

---

[12] He is writing shortly after the end of the Apache wars in the US and reflecting the then-popular harsh views of Indian behavior.

"You are wrong," said the jailer. "Here are eight women, exactly the number mentioned in my order. You can see for yourself. Here are the names."

"Nevertheless," said Maria Spiridonova, "there are two more women in this jail. I have seen them and heard them. You must set them free."

The jailer persisted in his denial.

"Very well, then," said Maria Spiridonova, "all go or none goes. Either you will bring out the others or we go back to our cells."

"There are no others, I tell you," wailed the jailer. "Here is the list, and here are the persons it calls for."

Maria Spiridonova turned about and led the others back to their cells. It was in the morning. Before sundown the jailer must have had before his eyes a convincing vision of the firing squad, for he surrendered, bringing out from another part of the prison two old women that had been there so long their very names and offenses had been forgotten at Petrograd. Then Maria Spiridonova and the nine others started for the railroad station 500 miles away. Part of the distance they must walk. The two old women had almost lost the use of their limbs. At first they could hardly make a mile a day.

It was for these reasons that although the Revolution began on February 27, Maria Spiridonova did not reach Petrograd until late May. She brought her two old women with her. All for one and one for all.

Little was ever made of the fact in this country, but the reformers also abolished capital punishment, which in ordinary times would be well enough. If there be any sense in the gallows anywhere, surely there is none in Russia. The Russian loves not violence and would seem to have little need of a vision of the hangman to keep him from it. In all the time I was in Russia I never saw a blow struck nor a serious altercation.[13] Even among great masses of idle soldiers I never saw such things. I did see thousands of soldiers strolling two by two with arms about one another; also, I did observe many a fierce discussion as to whether Germany or England really started the war, and the like. But when it was over the disputants usually walked off arm in arm. It might have been otherwise and far worse in the old vodka days; I do not know. I speak of it as I found it.

One of the most astounding changes was in the church. To those that knew old Russia nothing seemed so preposterous as a suggestion in those days that this institution of the ages could ever be made democratic. The old moss-grown Orthodox Church, unchanged and unchangeable for nine hundred years, rumbling forever around and around the same invariable ruts—if that can alter, men might say, let the mountains dissolve and the stars fall into the sea.

Yet the remaking hand of the new order touched even this sacred relic. While we were there a convention or convocation or something of the entire Orthodox Church

---

[13] This was a popular—but very wrong—idea brought back by many visitors of 1917.

in Russia was called at Moscow, and it hardly did a thing but rip old tradition into long shreds and cast it on the scrap pile.[14] No more domination of the church by the government, no more making of bishops and archbishops by governmental authority. Twelve bishops created by the Tsar at the dictation of the vile Rasputin were dismissed; their successors chosen by ballot. Hereafter all church affairs to be managed by a synod chosen by the votes of the people in the congregations, men and women voting together. Advanced education to be required of candidates for the clergy; no more ignorant priests. All church proceedings to be open and in the daylight; no more hugger-mugger and star-chamber business. The church to take by the hand any other Christian sect in any land and to work in harmony with it. No more sectarian bitterness; no more persecutions!

And next I tell you, as the strange fact with which to round out this tale of the impossible, that so far as I could learn nobody was opposed to this program of sweeping reform. It was not something put forward by young hotheads and sourly fought by Ancient Respectability. Everybody seemed to be in favor of it, just as everybody was in favor of the Revolution. For that is another strange fact. You could have passed the whole population of Russia through a sieve and not catch enough regret for the old regime to supply a mute at a French funeral. *Good riddance to bad rubbish!* sang the nation as it wrenched the shield of Nicholas II from the sides of the railway cars and cut the old Russian national anthem from all the music books.

In the church convention, convocation, or whatever it was, one of the prominent figures was a priest from San Francisco, Father Alexandrieff, a good man and able citizen.[15] The convocationers, whenever they got into a clove hitch about anything, fell to asking Father Alexandrieff what was the custom about such things in American deliberative bodies; for you must understand all this is new business in the church. So then Father Alexandrieff would state what was the American custom, and the convocation would think it a good idea and adopt it.

Democracy and equality for all—Jew and Gentile, Russian or what not, all on one plane! Against the somber memory of Old Russia, now dead and gone, think for a marvel of a Russia in which Jews are treated exactly like Gentiles! We have lived to see it, and it alone ought to crown the Revolution with imperishable glory. But, in truth, the hideous persecution of the Jews in Russia was never the will of the Russian people, but the work of the old ruling class that will never rule again.[16]

---

[14] The 1917 revolution allowed major religious reform movements, including the restoration of the Patriarch of the Russian Orthodox Church and the emergence of major religious reforms.

[15] A Russian Orthodox priest who had spent a long time in the United States.

[16] A little inaccurate about popular participation in Jewish pogroms. However, in 1917, the Jews' situation was much improved, and many played major roles in government and political parties.

For I think I will end this show of marvels by citing this remarkable fact, that even members of the old ruling class and some beneficiaries of it did not seem then to want the old order to return. I suppose the traitors, the trucklers and statesmen of the Tsar that tried to sell Russia to Germany were not of that mind because the fortress of Peter and Paul is an uncomfortable residence, and, capital punishment for treason having been restored,[17] there was still some hope that they might be hanged. But I mean the generality of people, including certain former noblemen out of a job.

On that Sunday in June when the great popular demonstration engrossed all Petrograd, armies of civilians and soldiers marched through the streets to show their devotion to the most radical conception of the Revolution. In the Nevsky a Russian friend called my attention to an ordinary-looking citizen strolling along the sidewalk with his hands in his pockets and his rather billycock hat somewhat on the back of his head, while he smoked a cigarette and looked with interest upon the moving throngs.

"Do you know who that is!" said my friend.

I did not.

"Well," said he, "that is the Grand Duke Michael, the late Tsar's brother, to whom he offered the throne."

Out in the street the people marched quickly along, borne up visibly by a new hope, their eager faces alight with it—men and women that six months before had been hunted like rats by the hounds of the old system or had clung to life in Siberian prison camps. On the sidewalk drifted this man, once so conspicuous, a piece of wreckage thrown up by the great new sea, unregarded or forgotten, as unregarded as the mechanic with whom he touched elbows and with whom he stood upon a plane of equality at last.

---

[17] Capital punishment was abolished by the Provisional Government, then temporarily restored after the July Days, but may or may not have ever been used during the time that he was there.

Chapter IV
The Old Regime and Its Fruitage

Because of the innovations on the new social program and because of the incessant misrepresentations dinned into our ears, it was a censorious view that most of us were inclined to take of New Russia. But after all, the wonder was not that some things did not go well but that anything went at all. We had no call to be amazed at some degree of chaos; the real wonder was that there was anything else.

According to all human experience and history the only normal state to follow the Revolution was maelstrom and whirlwind.

We were strangely prone to forget all this. An enormous hulk, the product of centuries of deliberate effort, had borne up the whole structure of organized Russian society. The eyes and minds of all men were always upon it; it regulated even the minutiae of their lives. In a moment this huge thing had turned turtle and gone down. Naturally it should have dragged everything loose in its swirl.

Always heretofore the violence of a Revolution has been attuned to the cruelty of the oppression against which it recoiled. It has been like a tree, bent over and then let go; it has rushed almost as far in the other direction. The oppression in Russia was the most savage, implacable, blood-guilty and maddening that has been known among civilized men, certainly since Caligula.[1] It was of the kind that relishes cruelty for its own sake; that develops an exquisite and dainty taste in cruelty. Thoughtful men, looking upon it, always felt that if it should ever be overturned, blood would surely have blood and anarchy would pay the price of a monstrous wrong built of murder and tears.

The world should never forget, no matter what else may happen in Russia, that in all these respects wisdom and prophecy went far astray. The Russian Revolution, when it came, was not only the least sanguinary of all great Revolutions in history; it was, all things considered, remembering its occasion and size, the most moderate, the least impassioned. The true story of those first days of emancipation has no reproach for the Russian people; on the contrary, it ought to be hung up for their everlasting praise.[2]

---

[1] A notoriously corrupt and incompetent early Roman emperor.

[2] He is speaking here of the February (March) Revolution and the great optimism that followed, not to what came after the time he was there, notably the Civil War and Soviet Union.

And it would be well if for all time another fact, here pertinent, could be impressed upon us. It is that without exception the features in the passing situation that had the severest criticism were every one the direct and sure result of the things the Revolution rooted out and of them alone. The evil autocracy did live after it.

Americans, it soon appeared, were particularly likely to overlook this vital point, and the reason was as before that daily they were treated in their newspapers to a diet of gloom concerning Russia. But if any of the dismal jeremiads of that day be now analyzed it will be found to be either something that never happened or something founded upon an aftermath of Tsarism. To this there is no exception, even to the Bolshevik counter-revolution of October, 1917; even to the imprisoning of the old ministry; even to the power and organization of the Bolsheviks themselves. If there had been no manifestation of this kind, reform would have rung false and the Russians would have been of such a make-up as to be the fit slaves of the next oppressor that might come along.

I will take as examples two of what were then the favorite themes of writers that loved to sound the harp of foreboding over these dark seas. One is what was called the mutiny or revolt at Kronstadt and the other the fact that after the Revolution Russian private soldiers generally ceased to salute their officers.

Kronstadt, the great Russian naval station, used to be one of the important defenses of Petrograd. The town lives on the arsenal, shops, ships and sailors.

When the Revolution broke the Kronstadt sailors and workers rose, killed some of the naval officers, imprisoned others and in the end declared the place to be an independent republic, not in any way answerable to the Provisional Government at Petrograd.

Superficially, of course, this looked very bad. It meant anarchy, disorder, chaos or almost anything else of evil. What could be hoped of a people that would do such things? The world, properly shocked, reading the despatches that dwelt at length upon these events, drew only the worst conclusions.

But the other side of the story was never told, and when that is known it takes on a very different look. For many years Kronstadt had been for the plain sailors of the Russian navy a most notorious hell on earth. In the fortress was a series of dungeon cells, far underground, unlighted, wet and infested with rats—the reproduction of traditional horrors of the early Middle Ages. For slight offenses or for none, for the whim, caprice, petty spite, or bestial pleasure of an officer, men were thrust into these places. Some of the cells, in frank imitation of a historic torture-chamber, were so built that the prisoner could neither stand in them, nor lie at length. Men condemned to these frightful holes sometimes died of their torments or went insane there without even knowing for what they were being punished.

There was no form of court, of trial, of hearing; no sailor had any chance for appeal or redress. It was like a chapter from the history of the Bastile; the first thing the poor wretch knew he was seized, ironed and flung into the dungeon. Indeed, in one sure respect the record of this place of villainies went beyond anything ever said of the Bastile. For the victim of the monstrous system of Monarchical France was always a person that some other person wanted to have out of the way; there was always a reason, however hideous, for the Bastile's atrocities. But Kronstadt is a chapter from the annals of human devilry, pure and simple. Its victims very often had offended no one. It was a principle, if so it can be called, of the naval service that the cells at Kronstadt must be kept full "for the good of the service," that the dogs of common sailors might know their place; that they might never forget the iron rod that hung over them; that being so cowed and so kept groveling they would always instinctively obey.

It was a theory that had not only sanction but high warrant, for it was exactly the theory upon which the government was conducted. Kronstadt was but an accurate reflection of the whole system of Russian autocracy. Dogs and beasts were the people and to be kept so. Who should care for the confinement of a dog? Who should care if a beast be beaten?

Where Kronstadt was not available the same exalted theory was carried out upon the ships. Men were daily kicked and beaten as part of the routine. Slight transgressions that in another navy would receive a reprimand, a word of warning or perhaps no attention at all, were here punished as in the old slave galleys. The idea that a sailor could have any rights or be entitled to any degree of justice was literally unknown.

Not all the officers of the Russian navy were brutes; there were thousands of intelligent and decent men, some of whom it has been my privilege to know. But the brutes were in the majority, were in sympathy with the theory and practice of the government, had their own lawless way, and piled up a terrible account to be settled. It was strange that they seemed to learn nothing from the sobering experiences of the Japanese War. The two Russian ships that in the great battle in the Sea of Japan mutinied and refused to fight, the four other Russian ships that mutinied and ran away, taught them nothing. Even the marvelous and tragic story I am to tell hereafter, of the cruiser Potemkin in 1905, which tutored all other spectators, even the gathering clouds of Revolutionary storm, had no message for them. The rest of Russian autocracy might seem to be cracking in those months from Bloody Sunday, 1905, to February 28, 1917, but the day of reckoning came around and found the reeking dungeons of Kronstadt as full as ever.

Likewise on the night of that memorable day they were full, but full now of other tenants.

At the crash of the Revolution the soldiers and workers of Kronstadt killed certain of the hated officers, and thrust others into the prison cells to which they had been so fond of sending helpless sailors. What would you expect them to do?

The independent republic at Kronstadt was a bit of serio-comic blundering like the ending of the Potemkin's cruise, but even that has its adequate explanation.

As soon as the Revolution came most of the existing local governments in Russia went out of business and their places were taken by Provisional Committees, which steered the machine until new city councils could be elected. The world has been made to resound with tales, real and fictional, of things all askew in Russia. Nobody has ever pointed out the fact that most of these committees, although made up of men that about such a business were greener than grass, turned off an exceedingly workmanlike job of municipal management.

Kronstadt, of course, went with the rest, only farther than many. Instead of a Provisional Committee, it put all the local power into the hands of its Soviet of Sailors' and Workers' Deputies, which immediately took command of the municipality.

Probably the Soviet was arrogant. Men suddenly swept out of a hideous slavery into great power are not usually noted for a sweet and lamblike disposition. Anyway, the Soviet sent word to the Provisional Government in Petrograd, demanding to be represented in its deliberations. The only notice the Provisional Government took of this was to send a man to represent it in the Kronstadt Soviet.

This was the worst possible blunder. As one of the Kronstadt men, who had been in America, put it to me, it was as if the Senate at Washington had refused to seat a Senator from New York, but had sent one of its own members to sit in the New York Legislature.

So they seceded, started the independent republic of Kronstadt, and walked their wild and picturesquely lunatic road until they crashed into the Cossack machine-guns that July day in front of the old Duma building. After which the Independent Republic of Kronstadt seems largely to have disappeared from these scenes.[3]

But naturally, overt events of this kind played directly into the hands of the restless German propaganda and after the first few days there was plenty of trouble, all of a familiar brand, being truly made in Germany.[4] German agents were at that time chiefly busy along the whole Russian front telling the soldiers that the Revolution's creed of public ownership meant an immediate division of all the lands, and if they wanted to get in they must be on their way home; but in the intervals of these employments time was found to push along disaffection at Kronstadt or elsewhere and of course, incessantly, to emphasize to the American and other publics the most evil aspect of every development.

---

[3] Kronstadt quickly emerged as a center of discontent and radicalism. Its sailors played major roles in the revolution, both 1917 and the October Revolution, and the following Civil War. Russell was there after the July Days temporarily reduced their influence, and his account reflects that. It is weak, however, if one looks at their overall influence in 1917. The Russian word is sometimes spelled in English "Kronshtadt," which more exactly carries over the Russian letters.

[4] Another example of the tendency to assert German activity inside Russia as a way to explain events.

Conditions of almost insane cruelty in the Russian navy that made the story of Kronstadt a certain fruitage of savagery were duplicated in the Russian army with similar results. When the Revolution came and the tension snapped, I think it is wonderful that far worse things were not recorded. Contemplating the real life of a Russian soldier under the old system I could never be astonished that soldiers ceased to salute their officers; the only thing that astonished me was that there were any officers left alive to be saluted. It is to be borne in mind always that military service in Russia was compulsory, army or navy. A Russian that did not like to be kicked had no chance to stay out of that service. Upon arriving at military age he was practically seized by the government and forced into a huge organization where he had fewer rights than a horse and a far worse time. He had in fact ceased to be anything human or vital and became a doormat upon which the officers wiped their feet when in good humor, and a block upon which they vented their spite when they were ill-tempered.

Those that have studied the strange records made by human beings whenever they have been in positions of unlimited power know well enough that cruelty is another monster that grows by what it feeds upon. Moreover, we are to take note here of the significant fact that most of the officers of the Russian army were of the aristocracy or the near-aristocracy. For generations that class had understood its security to lie in keeping the masses in a state of subjection, and the best way to do that was every day silently pointed out by the abominable government. It was to beat and terrorize them into abject humility.

The result was that if there was anything worse on earth than the Russian naval service it was the Russian army service.

In Petrograd I became well acquainted with a young man that was a type of the best there is among the Russian youth, stalwart, upstanding, intelligent and thoughtful. He was at that time a non-commissioned officer in the Russian army and I will set down here his experiences under the monarchy because they may be taken as a fair average example of stories I gleaned on every side and not open to question.

His family, although of the lower orders, was fairly well-to-do and he had been well educated. When the time came for his military training he was drafted into the infantry. A scoundrelly drill sergeant gave to him and other raw recruits about eight weeks of instruction, conveyed chiefly through the toe of the sergeant's boot vigorously applied and liberally assisted with curses. He was then put into a squad and employed to clean the officers' boots, empty their slop-jars and receive their kicks and abuse. He said that by some innocent oversight he incurred the ill-will of one of these officers. The next day at dress parade this officer walked down the line until he came opposite my friend and then deliberately spat in his face—three times. The soldier raised his hand furtively to wipe the spittle out of his eyes.

"What does this beast mean by raising his hand?" said the officer. "Take him to the guardhouse!"

So they took him to the guardhouse and kicked and beat him when they got him inside the door. Then they threw him into a cell to stay ten days—the first day without food or drink, the rest on bread and water. On the first day the officer came in, spat in his face, cursed him and kicked him. Two days later this officer brought in other officers to watch and enjoy this noble sport. It seemed to amuse them greatly.

He told me that many times he has seen maddening performances like this: at inspection or drill an officer would pass down the line and intentionally knock a soldier's cap sidewise.

"You miserable swine!" he would instantly bawl, "what the devil do you mean by standing there with your cap on crooked? Put it on straight instantly, and meantime I will give you a week's imprisonment."

The poor unfortunate wretch would now raise his hand to straighten his cap.

"Dog that you are!" the officer would shout. "What the devil do you mean by getting out of position? I will have you beaten within an inch of your life. Take this pig to the guardhouse."

Against this monstrous system, which had a million ramifications and variations according to the diabolical ingenuity of the torturer, the victim had not a shadow of redress nor hope. If he so much as murmured or protested he could be taken out and shot for mutiny.

The men were taught a formula of assent with which they were obliged to respond to every question by an officer, and the slightest variation in the words of the formula or its arrangement meant punishment. For instance:

Officer: "That is a spot of rust on your rifle, is it not?"

Soldier: "Sir, it is indeed, sir, as you say, sir."

If, instead of this arrangement, he should say "Yes, sir," or "Indeed, sir, it is as you say, sir," he would be punished.

There might be no rust whatever on the man's rifle and probably was none. He must nevertheless assent to the officer's statement. No matter how false it might be about anything he must still assent to it—in the formula I have mentioned, and none other. Occasionally at some kind of a hearing a private might be called upon to answer some question. No matter what it might be about nor how great the perjury, he must always endorse the office—in that same formula.

"The typical Russian," said my friend, "is sensitive and rather high-strung. Because he is high strung a little of this sort of thing will often confuse him, when in spite of himself he will be likely to commit fresh blunders. With the most malicious cunning the officers used to play upon the Russian susceptibilities and drive and nag their men into committing breaches of the rules that would bring down the heaviest punishments.

"The result of all this huge mass of evils, the beatings, kickings, imprisonments and terrible wrongs, was that millions of men in Russia went through life with an unappeased and almost insane hatred of the military establishment. Salute their officers? They had much rather kill them. What would you expect? The Revolution came and gave to many such men the chance they had dreamed of in long hours of torture and intolerable humiliation. Some of them went out and shot their officers, and the rest had inexpressible pleasure in abolishing the salute to the brutes.

"Of course all officers were not like this. Very many of them were courteous, decent, and kindly. You will find them still in the service, still obeyed and often still saluted. The brutes are dead or run away or gotten out of range. All in all, what seems to me the most wonderful thing is the small number we shot. When I think of what I saw in the service we seem either very forgiving or very forgetful."

In the same way and just as inevitably the futile attempt to manage the army through soldiers' committees, of which so much has been made in this country, was nothing but the normal outcome of the army under Tsarism. The soldiers had an instinctive feeling that they could not trust officers capable of so misusing their own men, and I have yet to find any reason to think the soldiers' feelings about this were wrong, unless we are willing to repudiate all records and assume it is not true after all that the bully is also the coward.[5]

But I may perhaps be pardoned if I once more insist that the bully in the army or the bully in the navy had at least this excuse—that whenever he carried out his atrocities upon the defenseless he was strictly upholding the favorite traditions and practices of his government.

Recording merely the facts and without seeking to advocate or oppose anything, it was here that much difficulty arose in trying to get an understanding between the people of the United States and the people of Russia. It was a psychological difficulty. We could not really sense the old Russian system as it really was. We were ready enough to admit in a general way that it was bad, but to know how bad it really was and to carry that knowledge always with us as the ready touchstone to lay bare every Russian mystery, that was clearly beyond us. Very likely it was beyond any people that did not know by the testimony of eyes as well as of ears the full measure of the old Russian government's depravity. For if we speak of descriptions, what words in use among men would be adequate to describe this, the achievable limit of evil and of man's inhumanity to man?

It was not merely a form of government belonging to an age in human history long ago outlived, and it was not merely a frozen horror crushing down upon the hearts and lives of men. It was also a vast and curious foundation for that government, carefully, cunningly built and developed by generations of astute minds.

In the end the base became by man's tireless ingenuity infinitely more wonderful than the thing it held up.

---

[5] Soldiers formed committees at the beginning of the February Revolution and they played an increasingly important role for the rest of the revolution. They were formed at all military unit levels in the army. Initially moderate and SR oriented, they became increasingly radical.

Every year, you might say, the governmental system of Russia demanded of wickedness a greater skill to keep it going. The task was to maintain a primitive despotism in an age moving swiftly toward complete democracy. The faster the rest of the world forgot the Stone Age the harder the task became to preserve a social system suited to nothing else. For some generations the character of the sovereign, arrogant, brutal and callous, helped out. When the throne fell to a half-witted little man [Nicholas II], as weak in will as in body, nothing is more wonderful than the expedients to which the real masters of Old Russia were driven to keep their ship afloat.

The two chief assets in the vast, elaborated and scientific business they built up for the minute supervision of people's lives were terror and ignorance. By maintaining Russia in a state of perpetual perdition for all persons that were suspected of favoring freedom it was possible to hold over all such minds an unchanging fear of a still worse perdition—which was Siberia.

People that know freedom, that were born in it, that have never known anything else, how can they grasp the meaning of this any more than a blind man can grasp the tones of a sunset?

Russia lived with a huge iron heel upon her breast. This was the marvelous police system, divided into three main organizations.

There was, first, the mounted gendarmerie, heavily armed, ready to ride down any manifestation of disorder.

Then there was the acknowledged city police, black-coated and menacing, chosen for physical strength and aptitude for cruelty. These were known and (with reason) feared of all men. There was scarcely a block in a city or town that was not watched incessantly by them.

But the true wonder, of course, began with the third division, or secret police, whose strange network of espionage wound itself around every hearthstone in Russia, peeped in at every window, listened at every keyhole. It was this that chiefly kept the Tsar's crown on his head and his head on his shoulders, year after year.

Let me see if by some examples I can convey to those that have never known anything of this kind an outline of life as it was under the Russian police.

Say that there were two friends among the Intelligentsia, the class most suspected and pursued. If they rode downtown in a trolley car of a morning, going to work or to business, they never dared to exchange more than formal salutations and sometimes not even these. If the car conductor were not a police-agent in disguise there was sure to be a police-agent lurking among the passengers. Almost any innocent remark dropped by either friend might be reported as of sinister import, entered against them in the colossal records that the police maintained, and used at any time as a fingerpost to Siberia.

In restaurants you must guard every word with the greatest care; the waiter is probably a disguised policeman. Be careful about your cabman; many police-agents have lately taken to driving cabs. A beggar solicits alms at your door; he may have been sent to overhear a disloyal expression or take note of your callers. Write your letters with scrupulous attention; they will probably be opened and read. Be most discreet about your telephone conversations; it is well known that every wire is tapped.[6]

Every educated man was particularly likely to be an object of suspicion. The mere fact that he was educated proved that he must know something about the outside world of progress and its opinion of Darkest Russia; he could not know that without some degree of discontent. Even in his own home such a man could never be sure any moment that the eye of a police-agent was not watching from some undiscovered hole, that the ear of a police-agent was not listening at an unsuspected cranny.

If such a man seemed to be of careful and unobjectionable walk, this sometimes served to make the police administration only the more suspicious of him, and then the agents provocateurs, the worst of all the instruments of evil, were loosed upon him. Someone in apparent distress begged his help and told a pitiful story of injustice or of police cruelty in the hope that he might drop an expression of sympathy. Canvassers tried to get him to subscribe for suspected journals, book agents tried to sell him proscribed books, and visitors dropped upon his premises Revolutionary literature that it might be found there and used against him.

He was likely to find at any time that his private papers at his home or office had been mysteriously rifled and yet he could never detect the stealthy person that rifled them.

The agents provocateurs often developed a depraved cunning that seemed superhuman and must ever remain a monument to mortal capacity of that kind. Many of the records of their deeds surpass any novelist's imagination. Their filthy business was to ensure outbreaks or overt acts that suspected leaders of the people might be trapped and the rest might be terrorized with the spectacle of a swift and awful retribution. They wormed their way into all clubs, societies and organizations, even when these were of the most innocent or benevolent character, took advantage of men off their guard and wrung from them evidence usable for their ruin. Among the secret Revolutionary and propaganda leagues they believed they had always members. These sometimes spent ten years in one organization before they were able to bring about the thing they were after. Very often they themselves would suggest, plan and help to carry out the assassination or bomb explosion with which they dragged down their quarry.

Most plausible, ingenious, skillful men and wonderful actors they must have been. When brother suspected brother and son suspected father they still managed sometimes to pass undetected in the most active Revolutionary circles. The world

---

[6] The various levels of police did indeed play an important and repressive role, but he somewhat overstates it throughout this section.

read with incredulity the confession of Azef,[7] one of their master-minds. Yet it is quite true that, as he said, he had worked at the same time with the police and with the Revolutionists, and had betrayed both. To win the confidence of the revolutionists he revealed to them the secret plans of the police, and then when time was ripe revealed to the police the secret plans of the Revolutionists. He brazenly avowed that he suggested, planned and took active part in the killing of the Grand Duke Sergius and then revealed to the police all the Revolutionists that had helped him in the killing.

He was but a type. There is not a question that the hideous system developed and maintained by Russian monarchy developed in turn new abysms of turpitude in human nature and new kinds of skill to carry out new and revolting inventions in crime. Compared with the horrible wretches that this system spawned and trained, Titus Oates and all the other historic scoundrels look almost respectable.[8] Treachery was everywhere; men inhaled it with every breath; they ate of it and lodged with it and went hob and nob with it along the streets. Life became literally blackened, cursed and poisonous with suspicion, and generations of freedom must pass before the human heart in Russia throws off the last of the most detestable poison with which every vein has been clogged so long.[9]

Turn then to the fact that in the midst of all these conglomerate horrors the Revolutionary doctrine was spread, the Revolutionary plans were laid, the ideas of advanced freedom and democracy were steadily promulgated, until Russia was at last made free, and I think there can be no doubt that this is a people of already great and memorable services to the cause of liberty and that their services are a sufficient warrant for confidence in their free future.

For we are to remember, also, that heroes and martyrs of liberty in other lands have struggled on in the face of death, but the Russians that wrought the emancipation of their country worked under the shadow of something still worse. When a spy's revelations had come, or the bomb had been thrown, those that were hanged were usually the most fortunate. The others, if they were leaders, faced shocking tortures first and Siberia afterward, and when Siberia meant the "cold katorga" death was always far more merciful.

Exile to Siberia had a wide variety of meanings. Thousands of men and women were termed exiles that suffered no greater hardship than to be turned loose in a wild, remote country and allowed nine cents a day for food, clothing and shelter. Because

---

[7] Yevno Azef was an infamous double agent, active in the SR party leadership while also a secret police agent. He had fled abroad and was living in Germany, where he died in early 1918.

[8] Titus Oates was a controversial figure in seventeenth century England who engaged in numerous conspiratorial and denunciation activities.

[9] Imperial Russia was indeed tightly governed, but he somewhat overstates it. He reflects a widely held view that he would have heard during his stay in Russia and which would have fit with his own outlook.

this was not quite unendurable and because of the stories of the amusements of the rich exiles at Irkutsk, the notion has spread about the world that Siberian exile meant no more than to be separated from one's home and familiar haunts. Some writers, who must have been singularly undiscerning, have even tried to shed a romantic halo about it, as if Siberia to a Russian revolutionist were about like France to a Jacobite. It was the men and women no more than suspected of Revolutionary sympathies that drew Irkutsk and exile within the fringes of civilization. Those that had actually raised their hands against the existing order fared very differently, and learned with lashes on their backs as they were driven into the mines or herded in huts in the Arctic Circle what kind of revenge unhampered monarchy takes on those that dispute its divine right.

There was, for instance, a camp just inside the mouth of the Lena River, reserved for the most detested offenders, where the tortures were so exquisite and fiendish that the principal business of the guards was to prevent the maddened victims from finding release in suicide. The place was so close to the North Pole that the Arctic night lasted for months. In this gloom the prisoners were not allowed to have anything to read nor enough artificial light to enable them to find in work any distraction for their minds. The demon that devised this torment certainly shot far beyond all the inventors of racks and thumbscrews, for the place was reserved exclusively for men and women of refinement and education upon whom its horrors would weigh most heavily. He judged aright, whoever he was; most of the victims went insane.

Looking calmly into the face of such a destiny, the Revolutionists, harassed by the police and surrounded by spies, went on with their propaganda and permeated the greater part of Russia with it. I do not believe the history of liberty has anything finer or prouder to show. Thousands of her patient, unselfish soldiers perished in that long fight and left not even the shadow of a name.

The world may take Siberia lightly; to anyone that knows the Russian history it will always be a word of tragic import. In seventy years there passed through one Siberian town on the sorrowful highway more than 800,000 exiles. You may judge from this fact how extensive was the police business of manufacturing terror. "When the sunlight of the Revolution broke upon this wilderness of despair every political exile and prisoner in Siberia was at once decreed to be free. There were more than 200,000 of them in Siberia and of these 20,000 were in camps and places so remote from the world of men that by July they had not yet been reached with the glad tidings. You may judge from this fact how truly Siberian exile was a living tomb.

Russians are among the most generous of people, tolerant, kindly and almost singularly free from any vindictive impulse. The day came when the men that had been responsible for all this red world of pain and misery, this "draining of eyelids, wringing of drenched hands, sighing of hearts and filling up of graves," fell into the power of the people they had wronged and tormented. Not one of the red-handed murderers, from the Tsar down, was injured in a hair of his head. The worst that happened to any of them was to be confined in a palace or a fortress. Even when indubitable high treason was added to their other crimes they escaped the firing-squad they had earned.

All except the police. It was the hated police that fought the Revolution. It was the police that mounted the rapid-fire guns on the roofs of the houses and mowed down the people in the Nevsky Prospekt.[10] All those buildings by the canals, around the Ministry of Agriculture, along the Morskaia and elsewhere that are pitted now with bullet marks, got their ornamentation because the people in the streets must fire at the police on the roofs. Those green graves in the midst of the sandy waste of the Field of Mars are filled every one with the victims of the police, and it was the police that the crowd beat to death and flung into the canals when the tide of the Revolution rose high enough to overflow the vicious old tyranny at last and deliver the oppressors into the hands of the oppressed.

The day of retribution had come. But it was only upon the police that the vengeance of the people fell. The hated black uniform had disappeared from the streets. When the battle on the housetops began to go in favor of the popular cause the rotten old police structure fell with a crash. Next day the ice in the canals was covered with the bodies of policemen, and all those still left alive had fled in disguise or were locked up in that island fortress to which they had dragged so many of their victims.

And the great, wonderful system of interwoven espionage, the great army of spies, listeners, lurkers, eavesdroppers, weasels, ferrets, hyenas, Black Hundreds, police-hounds, dirty dogs, human wolves, wire-tappers, and the rest—what became of all that?

It sounds like a tale of unreality or of magic, but the whole thing dissolved like a mirage. One moment it was oppressing all men's hearts with its scowling and unassailable front. The next, it had ceased to be, and the wolves, ferrets and hyenas it had nourished were in full flight. Great fear must have come upon them; very few have ever been found. Some got over the border in safety, to Sweden or Germany; many in disguise still hide in unsuspected holes; some, under assumed names, enlisted in the army.

One at least, even in the terror of those hot hours, did not lose his cunning. With one exception the only buildings the crowd destroyed were police-stations. A crowd with torches was marching from one station to another.

"Comrades! Comrades!" shouted a man, springing upon a doorstep. "On to the Justice Hall, on to the Justice Hall!"

So he led them to the great white building, the hated place whence so many patriots had been sent to Siberia, and they burned it to the ground and it contained

---

[10] This was one of the popular beliefs about the February Revolution, repeated in writing down to today. In fact, there was very little firing from rooftops, if any. Most shooting was done in the open and by various people, officials and others.

all the secret records of the police spies, who they were and where they lived and on whom they had spied.

The wolves, ferrets and hyenas breathed freely again. After that their identity could never be made known.

That was the limit to which the violence rose; the tidal wave of chaos normally due from so great a convulsion never arrived. Petrograd and all Russia lapsed into a state of acquiescent good order and good nature. The people had destroyed the old autocratic government; they took no interest in punishing the elegant thieves and scoundrels that had conducted it.

It was probably the worst government that ever existed on this earth. Autocracy is always rotten and always a curse; this was rotten beyond all previous records of autocracy and a curse that made the plagues of Egypt seem negligible. It contained men that had stolen the money appropriated for rifles and sent unarmed Russian armies to the front to be slaughtered. It contained men that for a price had betrayed Russian armies into places where they were caught and shot down like rabbits in a trap. It contained men that had stolen food from soldiers' lips and clothing from soldiers' backs. It contained men that had stolen cartridges from soldiers' belts and shells from great guns. It contained men that wallowed in millions they had stolen from taxes wrung from peasants and half-starved workers. It contained men that had agreed to sell their country to Germany.[11]

Not one of these was hanged.

Yet they inflicted upon Russia a plague that will long survive them. They and their kind crippled, broke down or ruined every part of the Russian government machine. They made it inefficient and incompetent beyond anything men have seen since the final impotency of the Roman Empire; they corrupted and stole and rotted and perverted until the thing stank and was nothing but the putrid shell of carrion. Since their day all the men that have tried to supply Russia with any form of government, whether Bolshevik or anything else, have been cursed and followed by the blight Tsarism left behind it. Whoever might be at the head of a department, his subordinates, or most of them, must of necessity be relics of the old days of incompetency and theft. No zeal or industry could in a month or a year cope with such conditions. Let a man be as capable an administrator as lives, he could not quickly displace all of the left-overs of the old system; he could not readily root up all the old methods and supply new. But from that very fact, in the railroad department, for one example, came, as we are still to see, a black flood of troubles and causes that made any stable government in Russia for a time impossible.

---

[11] He is referring here to two things. First, that in the early part of the war Russia lacked adequate arms and its soldiers were sometimes sent to the front without weapons, expected to pick them up from the already dead or wounded soldiers. Second, there was indeed corruption by contractors.

Into this situation stepped once more that ubiquitous pest, the German propaganda. For its work in disorganizing machinery and spreading discontent it was supplied with funds free of expense to itself. I was never able to satisfy myself as to the truth of the story that the plates of the Russian paper ruble were in Germany, but there was no doubt that Germany was sending into Russia counterfeit paper money that could not be detected from the genuine. Bales of this medium arrived and with it Germany paid her spies and agents and bribed her way to success. Russia was at that time on a paper basis. All gold disappeared with the outbreak of the war, all silver soon followed it, even copper small coins became scarce and imprints of postage stamps must be issued to enable change to be made. The ruble had sunk to half of its normal value. At such a time the art of the counterfeiter was a double advantage to Germany. It enabled her to carry on free of charge her tremendous underhand operations in Russia and at the same time create trouble by lowering the value of the ruble.[12]

Considering all these conditions, the restless activities of the element that believed a new epoch to have dawned on earth with the Russian Revolution, the mental attitude of a nation weary of war, it is not strange that the Provisional Government fell and for a time another order of mind [the Bolsheviks] secured the control of Russia. But besides all these factors there was still another that in any country and among any people at any time would have insured trouble, and that, being one of the profound causes of the collapse of Russia on the battle front, we are to treat next.

---

[12] Again, he attributes to Germany a very real problem that in fact grew out of Russian conditions and the war. Inflation had actually begun in Russia in 1915 and expanded rapidly during 1917 as the economy broke down and the government became unstable. It, including the increasingly worthless paper money the government printed, grew out of Russia's economic and other problems, not German intervention, and grew steadily worse as civil war began.

Chapter V
A Broken Down Railroad and What Became of It

One of the ablest of the members of the Provisional Government of which Prince Lvov was prime minister was M. Skobelev, Minister of Labor.[1] He was a civil engineer, young, well-educated and skillful, and his career had been romantic as well as exciting in the days when he had been a proscribed advocate of freedom. On a day in July, 1917, an American was sitting in M. Skobelev's office, chatting with him about the railroad situation in Russia, when the minister turned abruptly and plumped upon the American this somewhat startling question:

"Will you tell me what you really think, personally, in yourself, about the Russian democracy and its chances to survive!"

The American reflected for a moment and said:

"As to the democratic spirit in Russia, that I believe to be at least as fine, as high and as genuine as any I have ever found anywhere in this world, of which I have seen much.

"But as to whether it is likely to survive as it is in the existing conditions, if you will look down that street you will see the answer."

He pointed to where before a baker's shop stood in the street a long line of patient women.

M. Skobelev looked at his visitor inquiringly. "I mean this," said the American. "It is now summer and to stand there for hours in that line is merely irksome and tedious. When winter comes it will be a different matter. People that overthrew the monarchy may be willing so long as the weather is good to endure another government that fails to relieve their distress, but they will not endure it when they must stand for hours in the sleet, snow and bitter winds that you have in winter. More especially when they know that there is food in the country and they suffer only from a failure to distribute it. In other words, the life of the present system of government here depends upon the rehabilitation of your railroads. If you do not secure that you will have another Revolution when the snow begins to fall."

---

[1] Two of the most important men of 1917. Prince G. E. Lvov, a liberal aristocrat, became the initial minister president of the Provisional Government, and held that office until July. Nikolai Nekrasov was an original leading figure in the moderate socialists—a Menshevik—and joined the government when it was reorganized to include Petrograd Soviet figures. He remained an important government figure until the October Revolution.

The American was perfectly right. Soon after the storm of the Revolution had subsided it was evident that whether Russia was to have at once a stable and efficient government or was to go through another period of stress and tempest, lasting no one could say how long, depended then upon two things, the United States and a supply of box cars.[2]

As to the United States, the question was whether it would understand and sympathize with the efforts of a newly emancipated people struggling to erect a democracy, and as to the box cars, it was whether a considerable part of the Russian people was to have anything to eat.

Doubt as to the United States did not last long. The American Government showed that it could sympathize with such a situation and much of the American press showed that it could not—or did not. For every Russian that knew of the Government's sympathy a hundred knew of the hostility of the press and never heard the news about the Government; so to a great extent that issue went wrong.

The other hung for a time in the balance, and again it was the United States that was a considerable, though in the end a defeated, factor in the effort to solve a difficult problem.

A bread line, as I have intimated, is not at best a pretty thing nor any indication of strength. In Petrograd and Moscow that summer we had worse than bread lines; we had meat lines, vegetable lines, milk lines, shoe lines; almost everything the people required they must get by standing in line and waiting for fixed amounts of the commodity to be doled out upon a showing of cards.

Suppose a cold rain to be falling, fifty women, old men and children, standing there without protection, soaked and dripping, shivering in a bitter wind—the spectacle is not exhilarating. The women have cloths folded over their heads and tied under their chins; they have garments that seem to be thin and wraps that are surely inadequate. They stand there patiently, head cloths streaming icy drops like a winter's eaves, soppy wraps clinging to their forms—no, it is not pleasant. It was not pleasant even in the milder days of September. With the snows and frosts of November it became plainly fraught with the perils the American had pointed out. The suffering was keen and was unnecessary.

Bread by ticket, meat by ticket, fish by ticket, milk by ticket, potatoes by ticket, a handful at a time. It was as if Russia were starving and all the population must go on rations and save every scrap. It was as if the nation were in a state of siege and blockade, the enemy surrounding her and all her ports closed so that she might be cowed and subdued by gaunt famine.

Was it so with Russia, then? Not at all. There was no food shortage in Russia; taking her altogether she had an abundance of food. There was no blockade of her

---

[2] Here he begins to explore the very real problems caused by a transportation system that had been shifted to meet war needs and then simply began to break down. Many visitors noticed the shortness of goods in cities and long waiting lines described above.

food supplies; she fed herself and more. In that same summer of 1917 she was able to send great quantities of wheat from Archangel to England.

In Petrograd, Moscow and some other cities bread was doled out a crust at a time; not far away, as we are accustomed to count distances, the sacked wheat stood by the railroad track in long piles as high as a two-story house, some of it three years old. Meat on tickets, a pound at a time; and not so very far away the plains were black with cattle. Tool steel and metals at fabulous prices or unobtainable; and great quantities of all of them lying on side-tracks.

In Petrograd the prices of all necessaries were so high that poor people looked upon them with despair. Forty-Eight hours east of Petrograd no food product was dearer than before the war and there was a surplusage of all staples.

Here are some comparative prices I compiled while I was in Petrograd:

	July, 1914	July, 1917
Bread, a pound	1 cent	5 cents
Meat (av., retail) lb	9 "	45 "
Butter, a pound	25 "	65 "
Potatoes, a pound	1 "	6 "
Eggs, a dozen	12 "	30 "
Lemons, a dozen	30 "	$1.44
Nuts, a pound	11 "	40 "
Sardines, a box	5 "	20 "
Radishes, small, 10	2 1/2 "	20 "

A pair of shoes that would formerly cost 7 rubles ($3.50) now cost $25. For such a suit as one formerly paid $9 the price was now $60, and one must wait weeks to get it made. Such shirts as used to cost 60 cents now cost $3. Apples were 13 cents each and oranges 20. Go four hundred miles and you would find most of these things abundant and cheap.

Russia was not starving; Petrograd and Moscow were pinched for food, not because food was really scarce but because they could not get at it. The railroad system had broken down.

The world ought never to forget this, its most memorable demonstration of what transportation is to its modern civilization. It ought never to forget hereafter that transportation is its arterial and circulatory system; that if anything dams these arteries the body begins to shrivel and fall away to death.

The circulatory system of Russia was not only dammed, it was atrophied and maimed, with the result that the Government could not perform its functions and people could not get enough to eat. The right aorta of that system is the great Trans-Siberian Railroad, the greatest trunk-line in the world. When I was in Russia this vital artery was in a state partly paralyzed and partly bordering on collapse, and when you have learned what ailed it you will have learned what it was that next to German propaganda and Allied misplays brought about the Russian downfall.

Let us begin with the port of Vladivostok, which I believe presented in 1917 the most extraordinary spectacle of the kind ever known to man. When I was there nearly 800,000 tons of freight were piled up in and about the place. Some of it had been there for years and was rotting.

It was a sight to be remembered. The hills about the handsome harbor were covered with great tarpaulined stacks of cotton bales, most of them three years in that position. There it lay and doubtfully adorned the landscape, while Russia badly needed cotton. On the shore were 25,000 tons of automobile trucks and parts, while Russia badly needed automobile trucks and parts. Just outside the town was a bewildering pile of car wheels, beautifully arranged in a pyramid I should say 400 feet long, 100 feet wide and 14 feet high, and Russia badly needed car-wheels. Next to this was a pile of car-axles, also artistically arranged, thousands of car-axles peacefully reposing, while Russia badly needed car-axles.

Around the shores of the harbor were great stacks of munitions of all kinds, and Russia badly needed munitions; thousands of guns, and she needed guns; millions of cartridges, and she needed cartridges; tons of textiles, tool steel, copper, hospital supplies, machines, and she badly needed all these things.

Day after day the steamers from Japan and the United States had been bringing such commodities and depositing them upon the fringes of the bay. Warehouse after warehouse had been built to hold them and still they came faster than shelter could be provided. Streets near the wharves were lined with goods so long exposed to the weather that the packing-cases had turned black and were beginning to break open.

All because the railroad system had broken down.

At that time Russia was facing a coal shortage so grave that the factories were likely to close for lack of fuel. Yet there is no end of coal in Russia; she has some of the largest deposits in the world. At one place on the Trans-Siberian Railroad I have seen a cut driven into a solid mass of coal, a side-track in the cut, a train of gondola cars on the side-track and men standing on the vein and pitching coal straight into the cars. I do not believe you can find such a spectacle anywhere else on this globe. The coal lay in a solid black mass, not more than four feet under the surface; scrape off a little clay and there was the deposit as black as your hat. Mining there could be done with a scoop shovel. And yet Petrograd and Moscow were short of coal. The railroad system had broken down.

Had broken down, or had been broken down; that is the better phrase. It had gone far to ruin partly because thieves and blunderers at Petrograd had been trying to operate in the Twentieth Century A.D. a form of government that would have been appropriate for the First, or thereabout, but chiefly because the inside had been stolen out of the system.

For years the Imperial Government of Russia had been the wildest carnival of graft, loot, plunder and corruption ever seen in this world. Unscrupulous men went into the national treasury with grapples and dredges and came out loaded down with money that did not belong to them. It is a story without a parallel. The dull, incapable little Tsar sat on his throne and the thieves walked in and out of the money-box before his eyes and he did not know it; they could have stolen the watch out of his pocket or anything else he had except his mustache, without bringing him to a state of mental alertness.

Everybody was supposed to thieve; some men kept straight, but they were regarded as eccentrics and cranks, and were seldom recognized in the best circles. A book on Russian graft would be a priceless addition to the store of human knowledge. It would include one of the most stupendous tragedies ever known, for thousands upon thousands of men are now in their graves solely because the arms with which they should have been equipped were stolen by Russian grafters. Some adequate punishment may exist for the Government officers that sent men into the battle-line armed with wooden sticks instead of rifles, but it cannot be in this world.[3]

Among the things that went to wreck in those days of plunder was the Trans-Siberian. No part of the breakdown of the railroad system is to be charged to the Provisional or Revolutionary Government. I ought to make that clear. The democracy inherited all of its railroad troubles. It came in to find about one-third of enough equipment and no way to get more quickly, and it staggered under that problem to the end. The money that should have gone into equipment had been grabbed by the grafters.

Even before the war broke, the supply of locomotives and cars was far below par. War clearage makes tremendous drains upon railroads. Millions of troops must be transported, millions of tons of supplies are required to keep the troops in form. On every front the entire army is moved backward and forward about every two weeks.

The cars and locomotives that were swept off for this service in Russia left the rest of the system bare.

I believe the real story of the Trans-Siberian excels any other chapter in railroad history. I have never seen it in print, but I will try to give an outline of it here, for the sake of the light it will throw on the Russian problem, although I think it is also a good yarn on its own account.

It is the longest of railroads, 6,205 miles from end to end. It was born in the brain of an American, and by a most extraordinary turn in the whirligig of fate it was Americans that in the crisis of 1917 alone appeared to know how to keep it from tottering to its fall. The first suggestion of it was made in 1857 to the then Tsar, Nicholas

---

[3] This was a feature of the opening of the war for Russia, 1914–15.

I, by an American engineer.[4] He pointed out that the whole vast territory of Russia in Asia, a realm known to have the possibilities of wealth without limit, would always be undeveloped and practically worthless until it had rail connection with the sea, and he urged the building of a line across Siberia to Vladivostok.

In the reign of Alexander II the plan slept while that unfortunate Romanov tried to meet the rising tide of intelligence and Revolution by instituting reforms. The next Tsar, Alexander III, brought it out of its retirement and in 1891 decreed it, appointing his son Nicholas, the last of the Tsars, to begin the work at Vladivostok. Accordingly on May 19, 1891, the then Crown Prince appeared at Vladivostok pushing a wheelbarrow, and amid elaborate ceremonies and blessed by the Church, he dug the first spadeful of earth on the Trans-Siberian, easily the most useful thing he ever did.

At that time a railroad was already built from St. Petersburg to the Volga River and a little beyond. The rest was completed, in a fashion, in eleven years, which was good speed when one remembers the long and terrific Siberian winters. By 1902 one could get from St. Petersburg to Vladivostok, crossing Lake Baikal on a steamboat and journeying on another steamboat 400 miles down the Amur River. The rest one did on the new railroad.[5]

Nothing was now lacking to make a complete and operated line from Petrograd to Mukden and Manchuria except the link around Lake Baikal, and Russian engineers were at work upon that. Japan saw that the time had come to strike; if she waited longer Russia would have her highway in shape for the ready passage of troops to the east; and Japan let go at Port Arthur, beginning the war. It was Lake Baikal that beat the Russian armies and gave the victory to Japan.

The lake is called "Holy," but in no such terms did the railroad people refer to it when they were trying to get troops and munitions across it. According to the best surveys it has a length of 375 miles, is 50 miles wide and in some places 3,000 feet deep. It is walled around with sheer mountains, sometimes 4,500 feet above the surface of the lake. The rock is unusually hard, and that is where the trouble arose. Yet the conformation of the country is such that the only feasible route was by this lake. To get around it required miles of tunnels through the hard rock. Meantime, the line reached the shore of the lake on the west and left it at about the southeast corner, and passengers and freight were ferried between the two points.

This was a highly picturesque performance, but not exactly suited to the requirements of war. The lake is one of the coldest in the world. It freezes over in November and remains frozen until well into May, sometimes to the first of June. Ice nine feet

---

[4] There is a slight error here. Nicholas I died in 1855, so either his date here is wrong or he meant Alexander II.

[5] The description of Lake Baikal and efforts to cross or go around it are quite good depictions of a real problem that faced Russian and American aid in 1917–18. Here, he has taken a step back to the Russo-Japanese War of 1904–05, an event in which getting Russian troops across the lake affected the war effort.

thick is one of its pleasing products; another is a particularly vicious and unreasonable kind of summer storm. The thick ice is normal; the temperature gets down to 50° and 60° below zero and 40° is considered balmy. But the summer storm, which is sudden and angry, is just perversity and condemned by all right-minded men.

So long as the lake was open the ferryboats ran back and forth with much regularity, but winter soon stopped them. The Russian Government sent one of its admirals to Sault Ste. Marie, Michigan, to see how the far-famed ice-breaker was worked there. The Americans received him with gladness and showed him everything, including the plans of the ice-breaker. These he wanted to borrow, and the Americans let him have them. He took them to England, where a boat was built on the exact lines of the Sault Ste. Marie breaker, but the Americans, according to report, were never able to get their plans back.

The ice-breaker is a vessel of great weight and strength, with an overhanging bow and a powerful breaking wheel forward, worked with a separate engine. It slides upon the ice and breaks it down by its weight, while the whirling wheel smashes and grinds. It will break ice thirty-six inches thick.

So long as possible the ice-breaker would keep open a lane of communication between the two shores, and the troops and their supplies would move that way. When the frost began to manufacture the ice faster than the breaker could handle it, she was laid up and the Government put down rails across the lake and hauled cars across with horses and oxen.

But these were only freight-cars. For reasons of excessive caution the authorities would never risk passenger-cars in that way. The ice was more than four feet thick and probably would have held a train of Pullmans, but the authorities would take no chances on it. All passengers were transferred across the lake on sledges.

The course was diagonal and about sixty miles long. The passengers reached the shore of the lake in the morning, were packed into sleighs and covered with furs until not even the tip of a nose was visible, and away they went over the ice, one sleigh and one harum-scarum driver for each passenger. To see anything of the journey so bundled in furs was of course impossible, but the precaution was wise on more than one account. There were cracks in the ice a foot wide that the sleigh glided over and the horses missed, and competent authorities tell me that to look down upon them as one swept along was no real enjoyment, because they went all the way to the water. It took two hours to get half-way across, and there one stopped and had luncheon, with much hot tea, before one did the rest.

This was the arrangement for travelers, please note. The soldiers fared with no such luxury.

When they reached the lake they marched upon the ice and footed it across. If one froze or dropped from weariness, what odds? 'Twas but a beast that was gone. Here as everywhere else the attitude of the Government to its soldiers was that they were next below dogs, though at a long distance. Sometimes in a temperature of 60°

below zero soldiers were marched upon that ice. Luckily there was never any wind; there never is around that lake in winter, but wind or no wind the trip was nothing in the way of a holiday jaunt.

Even Russian soldiers could not march sixty miles a day, so the Government erected a series of shelters in the middle of the lake and presently had a city built there on the ice. There was for first-class passengers a fair hotel, where they had their luncheons and could stay all night if they wished; and for the soldiers scores of huts, regularly laid out in streets, a variety of cheap shops, and even places devoted to amusement and rum. The place was lighted with electric lights and presented at night as gay an appearance as was possible in any city squatted upon ice in the center of the coldest lake in Christendom.

When spring came the Government took its hotel, stores and huts apart, put them away on shore and started the ice-breaker upon its labors. Very often, even so late as May, it would be unable to get more than a mile from the shore. Whereupon the gangplank would be run out, the passengers would disembark upon the ice, stow themselves in sleighs that were carried on board for the purpose, and be whisked away toward the opposite shore. It was the romance of arctic travel.

Meantime, the Japanese continued to beat the Russian troops as fast as they stepped off the train and the Russian Government to make frantic efforts to get a track laid around the lake before the Japanese should be too decisively the victors. The Japanese won at this game and Russia had to suffer the loss of that part of the railroad in Chinese territory that she had built to carry through her connection to Pekin and the south. Japan took over that estimable slice of Russian wealth and thereafter looked straight into Russia's back windows, where she is looking today.

The Tsar's Government always arrived everywhere about a year and a half behind the schedule. When the Baikal lake ferry had thoroughly beaten the Russian armies the Government succeeded in eliminating it. The road around the lake was completed and thereafter the trains rolled from St. Petersburg to Vladivostok, as they were rolling in 1917.

Truth compels me to say much of it was rather to be described as deliberate progression than as railroad travel by our definitions. The weekly express did the 6,000 miles in twelve days; other trains in from eighteen to twenty-two. Through trains, first-class and second-class, were comfortable, but the slow trains were a trial to the Western nerves, there is no doubt of that. One of the mysteries of the road's operations, and they were many and dark, was the long stops made at every considerable station. This was true even of the express trains; of others it might be said that they seemed not so much to be stopping as to have taken root. I was never able to learn the real reason for these long delays, if they had any. For a leisurely traveler of an inquiring mind they offered this advantage, that they enabled him to explore most of the considerable towns along the route, but I judged from their remarks none of the travelers I met were of this order.

It is a strange fact and one I cannot attempt to explain, but while this Tsar's bungling government could no more operate a railroad than I could operate a theological seminary, in building a railroad it showed invariably a most excellent performance. There is no better-constructed railroad in the world, all things considered, than the Trans-Siberian. In one respect it surpasses all others, and that is in its bridges. The long steel bridges over the Volga, the Yenesei and other rivers amaze every traveler and, I am told, impress every engineer.

The roadbed is dirt ballasted, but wonderfully maintained. One thing I noticed particularly was the care with which drainage is provided. Deep ditches on both sides of the track must keep the roadbed dry at all times and largely immune against the action of frosts. The ties average twice the size of ours and are always in first-class condition. I examined thousands of them on different parts of the line and never found one that showed any sign of decay. When you compare that condition with an average American railroad, where half the ties are punk and you can pull the spikes with your fingers, the difference—so long as you are traveling in Siberia—is refreshing. It has a somewhat different effect upon you when you are traveling in America and happen to think of our accident record. Rails on the Trans-Siberian weigh 75 pounds to the yard, which is heavy enough for the kind of traffic they carry. Contrary to the general belief in this country, it is not a single-track road. About two-thirds of it was double-tracked at the time I rode over it. The line around Lake Baikal, for instance, is a remarkably fine specimen of double-track construction, much of the way through tunnels. Of course the whole system should be double-tracked and would be if the Tsar's Government had been either competent or honest. Among the curiosities of the World's Unpremeditated Exposition of Stranded Freight at Vladivostok were 800 miles of steel rails intended to carry on the doubletracking work. They had lain there so long that according to an American engineer they had begun to sprout. Some of the line had long been graded and ready for them, but there they lay. If they could have been put into place they would have relieved greatly the congestion of the road and helped thus to clear the economic clouds gathering to the west. But the rails could not have been released unless the whole problem of the choked harbor of Vladivostok were solved. There was no way to solve that problem except by first of all making Vladivostok an American port and to that there were believed to be great obstacles.

Meantime the road was doing only one-third of its normal carrying capacity and the hills and harbor shores continued to be covered with piled up bales and packing cases. Freight trains went out of Vladivostok with ten and twelve cars when they should have carried thirty or forty. The main reason for the deficiency was the shortage of locomotives and cars brought about by the corrupt old administration; but there was another reason in the fact that the old administration was stupid as well as crooked and had fastened upon the enterprise methods that would have hobbled any railroad.

A BROKEN DOWN RAILROAD AND WHAT BECAME OF IT 79

We in this country build our railroads rottenly and finance them thievishly but operate them marvelously. Russia built its railroads marvelously, plundered them magnificently and then could not operate them at all. Any man that had been three months in the operating department of any American railroad could have told the Russian administration that its system for the Trans-Siberian would not work.

The main line, Petrograd to Vladivostok, is separated into seven or eight grand divisions, each with its own chief and staff constituting a kind of independent sovereignty. There is the Ural, the Western Siberian, the Mid-Siberian, the Eastern Siberian, the Trans-Baikal, the Vladivostok, and others, to say nothing of the line through Manchuria, which is controlled by the Eastern China Railroad Company, a corporation that the government owns.

Each of these grand divisions is responsible to the national railroad department, but is more or less jealous of the other divisions and stands upon its dignity as an independent kingdom. Suppose a freight-car to pass out of the Vladivostok division and be lost. The commander of the Vladivostok line would indite a diplomatic communication of inquiry to the commander of the Eastern Siberian division and in the course of two or three months, if he thought it worth while, the commander of the Eastern Siberian would make a diplomatic response that he knew nothing about the matter. Similar diplomacy would then be employed to discover if the car were on the Mid-Siberian, or the Western Siberian, and finally in the course of two or three years diplomacy might discover the car or it might not, and meantime the shipper could tear his hair in vain.

Cooperation between the divisions was lame. Some chiefs used to try to evade repair charges by loading for another division the decrepit cars that were reasonably sure to break down. Whole trains of freight used to be held up for weeks without visible cause. When freight became congested there was no dominant central control to come in with the voice of authority and compel the tangle to be untied. Some of the division chiefs were solemn old boys that had graduated out of the army and existed apparently to move about in an atmosphere of antique and ponderous ceremony, and he that wished to obtain an interview with one of them must make motions like a man about to be presented at court. And some seemed not to care for the work in hand, but were firmly resolved to miss no pleasure as they went along and kept that resolution faultlessly, being one of the best things they did.

The whole concern was run as everything else was run under Tsarism, in a way forcibly to remind one of the way the old woman kept tavern. Since the war broke out I have listened to much learned discourse concerning the superior efficiency of the autocratic form of government. After a fair view of the greatest of all the autocracies and its works, that alleged superiority seems to me but of the stuff dreams are made of.

Except only as to the machinery of terrorism, never was a government in this world more absolutely inefficient and incompetent than the old Government of Russia.

The run divisions on the Trans-Siberian were about forty miles each. That is, an engineer started from Vladivostok, ran forty miles and stopped, he and his locomotive. The two then waited for a train coming from the other direction that they might haul it back to Vladivostok. There might not be such a train for twenty-four hours or thirty-six. Until then locomotive and engineer were out of commission.

This took about 35 per cent from the efficiency of what locomotives the road had, which were too few anyway.

Then there was no train-despatching. I think I see some American railroad man clutching the air in shocked protest at the statement, but it records fact. There was no train-despatching, or nothing that justly could be called by that name. Eleven telegraph wires ran by the side of the track all the way from Petrograd to Vladivostok, but they seemed from what I was told to have a function chiefly ornamental. A train started out and to its destination was entrusted to the care of Providence, assisted possibly by the ikons with which it might be furnished. If it reached a passing switch and the train it was to meet was not there it sat down and waited. Yet I am bound to say that accidents were very few, perhaps because of a system of blocking trains that had been imported from England and seemed to work very well—if one were not in a hurry.

Not much use was made of the telegraph, but the telegraph lines were well built and well maintained. In working them the operators used the old Morse recording instrument discarded in this country sixty-five years ago. It is very slow.

The road passes through some of the richest wheat land in the world, but there is not an elevator on its entire length.[6] The wheat is sacked, and the piles of sacks are covered with Chinese matting, and in this shape it lies by the side of the track awaiting shipment. Often it stays there until it spoils.

E. H. Harriman[7] journeyed over this line about 1905, looked at the black prairie soil, saw what it would do for wheat, concluded that here was the world's future wheat farm, and laid his plans to share in the certain profits. He intended to run a line of steamships to Vladivostok, to build elevators, to encourage immigration, to start the wheat industry and to haul the product. He died before he could realize his dream. Someone else will see it come true. Still, there is no denying it will be a hardy race that will undertake to cultivate this soil; temperature in winter 40 degrees, 50 degrees and 60 degrees below. In summer it is likely to be as bad the other way. We had 104 degrees in the shade crossing the Siberian prairies in July. The climate can only properly be described as brutal. Winter lasts until well into May; of a sudden you

---

[6] Here he is comparing agricultural systems, especially grain production in western Siberia and the American Midwest.

[7] E. H. Harriman was an American railroad executive whose visit to Russia inspired a railroad—agricultural idea. He died in 1909, before his notion could be developed.

A BROKEN DOWN RAILROAD AND WHAT BECAME OF IT 81

awake to find summer in full swing and the way the trees burst into full leaf seems supernatural. About twenty hours of sunlight daily cause the magic transformation.

But to return to the railroad, there is one good thing about it—you slide over it as a sleigh slides upon ice. There is very little jar when the wheels go over the well-made joints. Twelve days of the banging and hammering common on some American railroads would be insupportable to any except a man without nerves; twelve days on the Trans-Siberian are easy in that respect, anyway.

This judgment is not based on experience confined to the imperial train, either. From Vladivostok to Harbin we traveled, for a peculiar reason, in a train of the ordinary sleepers and they sailed with the same easy motion as the rest. The reason we had these cars and not the imperial train was because the imperial train was delayed on its way down from Petrograd to meet us. And the reason why it was delayed was because as it went along the peasants recognized the Tsar's car and got the idea he was in it and making his escape. So they compelled the train to stop while they searched it, and in the search they stuck bayonets through the curtains and broke open the closets until it was necessary to take that car out of the train and leave it behind. This little incident again may teach the uninitiated how much substance there used to be in those sweetly touching tales with which we were so liberally refreshed about the affection of the people of Russia for their ruler.

So we did not have the Tsar's car, but from Harbin on we had the rest of the Imperial train, including the car with the drawing-room where he used to play cards and where he signed his abdication. There on an evening on our trip, the representatives of three democracies were wont to sit comfortably about the table on which with some pen marks had been compassed the downfall of the greatest autocracy on earth. Amid all the triumphs of a bizarre and half-insane luxury I believe the thing that most impressed us was the Tsar's game table in this room. He must have had a liberal, not to say an abnormal, taste in the matter of games. The table was an imposing device that opened in the middle and being opened displayed two big boxes, one on each side. These in turn showed the makings of almost every game of chance known to man. There was a roulette wheel, a faro layout, poker, fantan, dominoes, backgammon, bridge, seven-up, rouge et noire, monte, Italian and Spanish cards, handbooks on different games, and checkers and chess. There were six or eight different kinds of dice and all the facilities for the ancient and unhonored game of craps. There were gaming devices that none of us could recognize, markers, counters and scores, from inspection of which it appeared that on the last occasion the outfit was used some imperial wayfarer was being badly stung, but we could not make out who it was.

The rest of this car was occupied by the dining room, with but one table, and that placed lengthwise, comfortable chairs and an elaborate service. The kitchen was still another car and occupied the whole of it. The staff there included a butcher, who used to slaughter for the imperial palate as the train went along, an arrangement rather desirable, it is to be supposed, in a country where there is no refrigeration and the temperature climbs to 104 degrees in the shade. There was also a car for the imperial baggage and two cars filled with armed guards, one at the head of the train and one at the rear, and these also were advisable lest the simple peasantry show in too explosive a manner how they really felt toward their dear Little Father.

The Trans-Siberian journey is like a visit to the human menagerie. Specimens of many strange races of men are exhibited first and last before your wondering eyes. Queer Chinese, still wearing the queue, paddle about the harbor of Vladivostok. The city is oversupplied with Japanese, men, women, officers, and soldiers. Feeble Koreans, that act as if they were about half-famished and have unhealthy-looking little beards, swarm in the outskirts. At some of the stations there are Turks. Harbin is one of the strangest places on earth and a babel of polyglot; I think every tongue is spoken there except Winch and Scandihoovian. In Manchuria the stations swarm with the Buriats, a Mongolian tribe that insist upon wearing the clothing of their great-grandfathers and are religiously opposed to taking it off or having it washed. A little further west, as before observed, the Buriat is a bandit and adds infinitely to the interest of life by seizing towns and kidnaping travelers.

At Udinsk is one end of the great caravan trail that stretches far down across the Gobi desert, famous in song and story, to Pekin, and casts upon this strand of civilization many unusual species of men. Then there are Kurgesi and Hindoos, Big Russians and Little Russians, White Russians and Cossacks.[8] In the summer of 1917 there were also thousands of Austrian prisoners tramping about in uniforms all in rags, thousands of German prisoners with their bright facings all gone tarnished, belted and tunicked peasants, and illimitable swarms of Russian soldiers, eating sunflower seeds and not otherwise having visible occupation.

A railroad station of ample size, concreted and whitewashed, the red flag flying above it, the walls adorned with red streamers bearing Revolutionary mottoes, the floors and platforms covered with the husks of sunflower seeds, soldiers, peasants, Buriats, bandits and what-not sleeping in the third-class waiting-room, where with the odors of ancient Buriat and of his clothes the air defied laws of physics and had become a solid; soldiers sleeping outside in the shade, soldiers in dense masses walking up and down oppressed with a visible boredom; all the railroad people in uniform caps, clerks, hostlers, yardmen, everybody; the town about half a mile away and thrusting above the white birches blue or green church domes shaped like turnips upside down—that was a typical station on the Trans-Siberian, where there was any town at all. This was not often enough to grow tiresome, I may assure you. Far more often there was nothing but a small brown wooden station-house, a dwelling for the employees, the switches for the side-track with which the trains pass, and the vast

---

[8] Little Russians was a name of the time for what are today known as Ukrainians. White Russians are the Belarus. "Big Russians" are the "Russians" of today. Little and big reflect numerical size. These three closely related groups are the three East Slavic peoples. I have left his spelling and descriptions of others alone.

level green prairie stretching away to the horizon, carpeted with exquisite wild flowers, just as our prairies were fifty years ago.

An immense part of Siberia reproduces North Dakota: the same level plain, the same black soil, the same beautiful carpet of green and gold and red and blue, about the same climate, only more of it, the same marvelous capacity for growing wheat, the same peculiar blue in the sky, the same tonic wine in the air. Yea, and by the soul of man, the resemblance goes still further, for in Manchuria, leaning meditatively against a station wall, I have seen a North American Indian, and more than one of him.[9] There he was, unmistakably; the high cheek-bones, the copper tint, the black hair, the piercing eyes, the arched nose, and they even tell me he has habits and instincts like the aboriginal American! There was not a doubt of it, we had come upon the cradle of a race; the Kuril and Aleutian Islands were the road by which he had traveled; and from where we were to the Penobscot and beyond, half way round the world, he had wandered and populated a continent. There may be stranger things in the human story than the relation of this spot to America and, as events fell out, of America to this spot, but I do not know what they are.

I spoke a moment ago of the huge masses of listless, unemployed and bored soldiers that one saw all along the line. That was another curse laid upon poor Russia by autocracy. I have long been convinced that God hates the autocratic form of government, the penalties for tolerating it are so many, so varied and so terrible. This was one of them. At the outbreak of the war the wondrously incompetent Government called out 14,000,000 men. What it thought it could do with them is beyond the fathoming of the finite mind, since it had rifles for only 1,800,000, and the second Russian line was armed with the wooden sticks I have mentioned before. Not only so, but great numbers of men thus armed were sent into the battle of Tannenberg and slaughtered like cattle.[10] There was not then nor at any time later in the war employment nor room at the front for so many men, but the Provisional Government, which was in control when I was in Russia, hesitated to demobilize the superfluous men because it knew the fact would be hailed by the German propaganda as heralding the Russian collapse. Also, very likely it lacked the decision to make this or any other radical motion and so drifted inert down to the cataract and over it. There is an interesting speculation whether if it had sent home the useless part of its army it might not have survived for a time with the rest, but this is profitless.

Of what autocracy meant to Russia and what were the inner soul and sense of it, there was in condensed form an excellent illustration in that over-decorated and

---

[9] North American Indian ancestors did indeed cross over from northeastern Siberia to Alaska. He did not see a North American Indian at this time, however, whatever the resemblance.

[10] His numbers and timing are off. His 14,000,000 comes close to the total mobilization throughout the war. In 1914 it was much smaller, although there was indeed a shortage of arms in late 1914 and 1915. By 1917 the Russian army was much better armed.

over-upholstered train we occupied. It had satin hangings, silk curtains, thick silk carpets, easy-chairs, lounges, bookcases, writing-desks, clocks, barometers; money had been spent upon it without stint and without reason. We sat at ease in it and rode past thousands and thousands of the people whose toil had furnished all this and who now stood patiently waiting for hours for their own poor train that did not come. Or we sat in easy-chairs and floated past such people roosting upon the wooden benches in the rude conveyances, no better than cattle-cars, that dull-brained autocracy had provided for them. And we rode past the wheat piled house high, the potatoes rotting in the fields, and the cattle browsing in huge herds over the hills, to Petrograd, where the people stood half of each day in bread lines, meat lines, milk lines and potato lines.

The money that should have provided transportation for these things had gone into silk curtains, satin lounges, easy-chairs, kitchen cars, guards' cars and the rest for a family of half-witted parasites that the form of government had saddled upon the country. Into these things and into the pockets of a horde of grafters and pilferers that the parasitical system maintained and protected.

Against the fruits of all these iniquities, which it had inherited, the Provisional Government was making a desperate struggle, ably assisted by the Stevens Commission of American railroad experts.[11] So great were the exigencies of the times that the work of this most able commission, which at another period would have been of world-wide note, was obscured from sight and never received adequate attention. The men that composed it were more than efficient railroad commanders; they were at once of recondite learning in their profession and of unusual character as citizens. They gave to the cause of democracy at a very critical time a most unselfish and ungrudging service. That Mr. John F. Stevens, the head of the commission, should have stayed on in Russia many months after the Bolshevik revolt, clinging still to the slenderest hope that his plans might be put into operation and Russia saved from the economic disaster that threatened it, was but typical. When we add the fact that Mr. Stevens' health was not good, that he was believed to be in great physical danger from the civil war raging about him and that he was neglecting at home all his personal interests, he seems to have deserved as well as any general on a battle field.

There was much and reasonable patriotic pride in this commission. One night at the Winter Palace while I was there, Mr. Henry Miller, a member, sat for an hour and talked of the condition of the Russian railroad system, and his discourse was a thing to cause a philosopher to ponder, for he spoke with such a command of language as only the cultured compass, with a technical mastery of every detail of his subject that could only be attained by years of specializing, and with the quiet dignity of him

---

[11] The Stevens Commission, headed by John F. Stevens, was sent from the United States to help get the railroads working better, which was essential for Americans to play a role on the Eastern Front as well as Russian war efforts more generally. Stephens had played a major role in US railroad building and in the Panama Canal.

that keeps his reserve power intact. On reflection I was led to doubt very much if any other country could have produced a man so variously endowed and that doubt I still entertain.

The impatience of the Bolsheviks, the great force of the German maneuvers in Russia, the reactions from the bread lines and the meat lines, and the mangled manner in which the cause of the Allies was presented, overwhelmed the country before the poor old Trans-Siberian had a chance to profit by the excellent plan of rehabilitation drawn by these skillful men. Yet some day it will be put into operation. It is to be hoped that when that day comes the authors of it will be remembered with at least a part of the credit they deserve.

Chapter VI
The Part Played by the Russian Women

At the news, which came forth in the summer of 1917, that the Russian "Battalion of Death," formed of women soldiers, was actually going to the firing-line to kill and be killed, the rest of the world seems to have gasped, half astonished.[1] Nobody was astonished in Russia. There, to the wise observer, it seemed perfectly natural. The Russian woman had no more than found a new field for her capable mind and restless energy. Why be astonished?

She was but bent upon making more history, which may be said to have become almost a specialty of hers and a line in which she has few superiors. She made a thick and unforgettable volume of it February 28 to March 2, 1917,[2] for instance. Then it was she that thrust in the lever, overturned vast rooted empire, and shot the once Imperial and Gracious Majesty from the seat of his fathers. She did it, the woman of Russia. After all the years of Revolutionary talk, dreams, hopes, and propaganda, hers was the hand.

The time, of course, was ripe for the fall of the house of bondage. With a savagery unequaled even in its own savage story, Russian autocracy had suppressed the Revolution of 1905, and made itself the historic sign of loathing so long as men shall read its record. New born democracy seemed to have been drowned literally in a sea of blood upon which the Tsar sailed more secure than ever. But all the time those that watched with any care the inner workings of events knew that the days of absolutism in Russia were numbered. Incessant labor, indescribable sacrifice had made all things ready for the last scene of the tragedy, but it was the women that rang the signal and furnished the greater part of the initial action.

The snow was deep in the streets and the cold was brutal. It always is brutal, all the way from November to May or thereabouts. Long lines of women were standing in front of the bakeries and meat shops. To wait in line for your daily food is at any

---

[1] The Women's "Battalion of Death" did indeed have a major international impact, although a very small military one. It was, however, a unique feature at the time and some will argue it may have impacted future women's roles. See more on it toward the end of this chapter.

[2] His dating here is confused or incomplete. The February (March) Revolution ran from February 23 to March 3 by the Russian calendar and March 8–16 by the Western one. The women's role was mainly in the beginning, but it was significant.

time in any place irksome business. February 22, [given the] latitude of Petrograd, which is one quarter of a degree from the Arctic circle, waiting in line is long-drawn torture and no better than man-killing—or woman-killing. Sometimes they light fires at the street-corners of Petrograd to keep pedestrians from freezing. There were no such fires along the hundreds of bread-lines that morning; and as to freezing, the women took their chances.

Of a sudden, in a side street just off the Nevsky Prospekt,[3] it struck some of the women that they had had about enough of this. With no more than a vague impulse of protest, they broke out of the line where so many mornings they had stood in sheep-like patience, and started down the street crying: "We want bread! Give us bread!"

They had touched the right string. At every corner other women flung themselves out of the lines, fell into step, and added shrill voices to the chorus. Other people peeped through their double windows at the strange sight, then tore downstairs to join the procession.

It was a bold thing to do; they were facing almost certain death. They knew it well enough; they had not forgotten Bloody Sunday, when just such a crowd, only much greater, had done what these women were doing now, and seven days afterward the snow in the square before the Winter Palace was still dark with their blood, a saving sacrifice to his Imperial Majesty, Nicholas II, Tsar of all the Russias.

And now women were crying it again, that cry of deadly peril, spite of Bloody Sunday, spite of all memories of the red blotched snow. "We want bread! Give us bread!"

The police, the hated blackcoats, ran hotfoot to put down this sedition among the Tsar's patient sheep. The mounted gendarmes came to ride over them. In five more minutes, according to precedent, it should have been over; some women shot, some women sabered, some women trampled to death under horses' feet, some women dragged to jail—and all well again. So many women, so many sheep. Peace reigns again in the happy sheepfold of the Tsar of all the Russias, gracious and benign. Sing, all of you that survive, God Save the Tsar!

---

[3] The revolution actually began February 23 (March 8) across the river in the Vyborg district when female industrial workers marched out of their factory and went to the nearby men's factories and demanded that they come out and join them in demanding bread and peace. It resumed the next day and spread to other areas, most importantly across the Neva River into the center of the city, especially Nevsky Prospekt, the symbolic center of the city. As most of the city went into demonstrations, the government realized that it needed to take action. On February 26 some soldiers shot into crowds, but then that night in their barracks, they decided not to do so again. When officers came for them the morning of the 27th, they revolted and went into the streets to bring other regiments out. By the end of the day, the revolution had in fact succeeded. His account of the beginning of the revolution is a somewhat romanticized one. Note that he was not there and learned of it only from people who were and had various versions, often emphasizing their roles.

But this time it did not result according to formula and well-known custom. Soldiers of the Petrograd garrison had come upon the scene and taken a hand in the playing. With grim oaths they swore they would kill the first policeman that laid hand upon one of these women. A blackcoat slashed with his saber at a woman's head. Bing! went the soldiers' rifles. The policeman fell dead, the other policemen fired back—the Revolution was on!

The Russian woman had brought it on, and now with conspicuous courage she bore her part in it. Beyond all doubt she is a good sort; she has character, resolution, and courage, no end. There was hot fighting that day up and down the Nevsky Prospekt, at that big red arch leading into the square of the Winter Palace, in the Liteinia, in other streets. The police knew their game; as before, they got upon the house-tops with their machine-guns. Soldiers and armed Revolutionists fired at them from the streets below.[4]

Where did they get their guns—the suddenly made citizens? The soldiers, I know, helped them to some, but the surplusage must have come out of subcellars, from behind old attic beams, out of carefully covered holes in the wall, where even the always watching, sneaking, stealthily creeping police agents could never find them; and now they were brought out by the women that had cleverly hidden them away. Women appeared everywhere in that fighting, Joans of Arc, unheralded and unsung. Women urged the men on, exposed themselves recklessly to the streams of bullets from the machine-guns, helped to build and defend the barricades. The stories of the eye-witnesses always include something about a woman that snatched a gun from a hesitating citizen and fired it, or some startling deed of that other heroine never sufficiently celebrated, that woman of activity so tireless and traits of leadership so obvious that the soldiers instinctively saluted and called "Comrade Captain."

The fight went on for hours. In the afternoon it began to go against the blackcoats. Soldiers tired of pot-shooting from the streets and got to the house-tops, where they drove the police from building to building. Sometimes they would corner a group and pitch them into the streets, living or dead. The people below, men and women, would seize them and throw them into the canals: living or dead, in they went.

Retribution for generations of hideous wrong. Probably no men upon this earth were ever so hated or so well deserved to be. They were the prize, pet, and selected blackguards of the world, sifted with care for every quality that can most make a man hateful. They licked the boots of place or authority, and upon weakness, misfortune, or revolt vented a horrifying cruelty. If even the gentlest woman was that day rejoiced by their fate, you will understand why. Revenge is utterly alien to the Russian character, but to execute justice upon the Russian police system would be in Russian eyes only a solemn duty.

---

[4] The shooting from the streets up at police or belief in them is true, although he exaggerates it, as most did. There was little—if any—shooting of police guns from rooftops, but the legend developed immediately and still is found in writings about the revolution.

THE PART PLAYED BY THE RUSSIAN WOMEN

This active part the Russian women played in the final uprising is what anyone that knew them would have forecasted. From the beginning the women have been the soul and chief inspiration of the Revolutionary movement.[5] In some ways it owes more to them than to the men; the women had usually the higher ideal, the greater readiness for sacrifice, the more dogged and dauntless persistence. So it will appear when some day this marvelous record is made up, but even now whoever has been privileged to talk with the women of the Revolution feels and knows that this must be the truth.

They had eminent need of all fortitude, for nothing, I affirm, was ever known in this world that demanded higher qualities of courage and capacity. The Revolutionists fought against the full strength of the most powerful of all autocracies, the greatest and most ruthless police force, the greatest network of cunning spies. Few Revolutionists ever felt the luxury of completely trusting anybody. The most fervent and active Tsar-haters by their side might be agents of the police; their own brothers and sisters might betray them.

It is agreed on all sides that in those long years of darkness and misery, women were the strongest element in the movement. Women were the dauntless and most efficient purveyors of the furtive propaganda.

Over the washtub or the soup-kettle, they knew how to convey information to other women in ways the police could never detect, and at night the women that received it whispered it into the ears of their husbands.

Men, they say, sometimes became discouraged; the thing looked so impossible for our time, so hopelessly far off. But the women kept on and knew not the meaning of dismay. The world has no fair knowledge of what they went through and probably never will have. Hundreds were put to death. Thousands were sent to Siberia, that place of darkness and tears. But not hideous Siberia, nor beatings, nor chains, nor the ingenious tortures of human-fiend jailers, nor starvation, cold, nor loneliness in prison cells, that potent devil to cow stout hearts, ever conquered the soul within them. Loneliness might kill them. It is recorded that scores died of it; but it never chilled their faith. As fast as one was hanged or swept away to exile, another arose to take her place and repeat her deeds. On the day that Sophie Perovskaia[6] was hanged for the killing of Tsar Alexander II, the police brought in three women for plotting to kill his successor.

The world marvels at the story of the "Babushka," the "Mother Catherine," of the Revolution, of whom I have spoken in another chapter, but when you come to

---

[5] Women played a significant political role, greater than any movement in the West, but he does overstate it. This exaggeration dominates this chapter.

[6] Sophia Perovskaia was a female early revolutionary who participated in the assassination of Emperor Alexander II in 1881, for which she was among those hanged. For that she became a famous figure in the Russian revolutionary tradition.

know what the Revolution really was she seems only its logical expression. Amazing woman—with the sweet face of a saint and the soul of a warrior indomitable! Where outside of Russia will you find another story like hers?

After years of successful Revolutionary propaganda carried on in the subcellar and attic as was required of such agents, the police got her at last and immured her in the cold tomb of Siberia—for life. She did what few of their victims ever did; she managed to escape, to make her way through a bleak and horrible wilderness to safety and finally to the United States. Here she had everything that should have made her contented: peace, security, the undying affection of thousands of friends. She put all these aside to thrust her head back into the lion's mouth because the restless spirit burning within her would not let her do otherwise. Friends wasted upon her their arguments and appeals; she resolutely turned back to Russia. Most persons could never understand why she should be so indifferent to the consequences. She was a Russian woman; that tells all.

She went back to the Revolution. In a few weeks some spy detected her. A day or two later she was traveling once more to the Siberian dungeon from which she had escaped. She was happier then than she had been at any time when she was free. She sang songs and was glad and warm within. She felt now that she was not enjoying security and comfort while others suffered for the cause, that she was bearing her part and taking her share. Nothing could be more Russian or more typical of the Russian woman, and in spite of all that has happened since, I cherish still the belief that of her manifestations the world may well take heed.

She went back to Siberia as to her grave, assured she would never taste freedom again. Ten years later the Russia she suffered for suddenly cast off its shackles and stood forth free, and all political prisoners being released wherever they might be, Mother Catherine was returned to the sunlight and free air.

It was a wonderful day when she came again to Petrograd. New Russia regarded with peculiar reverence all the heroes and heroines of the Revolution, but reverenced none so much as the "Babushka," the little grandmother. Dense crowds filled all the streets she passed. I think they wept as much as they cheered. This dear old soul that had endured so much and so long for their freedom, the absolutely fearless soul that walked smiling through the most appalling perils—and now come back to life. Perfect types of Russian Revolutionary womanhood, Mother Catherine, Vera Figner, and that most extraordinary figure of all, Maria Spiridonova.[7] I think we may chal-

---

[7] Important women revolutionaries. Maria Spiridonova assassinated a tsarist official, spent several years in harsh prison until freed by the 1917 revolution, and then became a prominent leader of the Left SRs in 1917 and 1918. Vera Figner was among those planning the assassination of Alexander II, and as a result spent a long period in prison and Siberian exile; she returned in 1917 to great celebration, but her role in the major political movements was less than Spiridonova's.

lenge history to produce their analogues, and yet how many thousands were there in Russia of a spirit exactly like these!

Such women now have the vote in Russia and will have much to say about the shaping of events there. Perhaps the reason why America so long refused to believe that woman suffrage was achieved in Russia was because it was achieved so easily. Our conception of woman suffrage is a great and precious boon that in a few places has been grudgingly bestowed after long struggle, and elsewhere may possibly be won by other long struggles—say some centuries hence. Russia had a different view of it. In Russia equality and justice for women were looked upon as the only normal condition, and the regions where women were excluded from public affairs were the anomaly—and portent.[8]

When the country came to elect the delegates to the Congress of Soviets and women voted on the same terms as men, nobody dreamed of any other arrangement; freedom was for all, not for a half of the population. Women voted in the remote parts of Russia and Siberia, peasant women that until March 1917, had been regarded by the gracious ruling class as the lowest herd of all the sheep in the imperial fold. And now they came forward to choose delegates that should hold in their hands the lives of the once ruling class and the future of Russia.

The best known of the five women delegates that sat in the Congress of Soviets was Lydia Rabinovitch, then aged twenty-four.[9] I heard her speak once on world peace, and if I could judge from the translation that one of my Russian friends whispered in my ear as she went along, it was a wonderful speech. Certainly its effect upon the audience was electric. She spoke with excellent wit, self-possession, and skill. As before remarked it was a difficult hall to speak in, because it was so disproportionately long. When I stood on the platform, it seemed to me the last man down there was a mile and a quarter away. But even he heard Miss Rabinovitch.

It may be taken as some indication of what was at that time the prevailing attitude of this country toward Russia that when the story of Miss Rabinovitch became known here it met with some incredulity and a general questioning as to how in an illiterate country she could have learned her command of language and her skill to make an effective speech. In point of fact she was a university graduate, spoke French

---

[8] He is describing a truly groundbreaking situation, where Russia became the first major country to give women full and equal vote. That had just been achieved around the time he arrived there, so it was a very public event for visitors from countries—including the United States and all the major warring powers—who visited Russia in 1917. All the major parties had prominent women members, but he does overstate women's influence politically.

[9] Note that there were only five women among the hundreds of delegates. Lydia Rabinovitch was someone who made a big impression on him, but not on other visitors and historians, and she soon disappeared in writing about the revolution. Unfortunately he does not name the others, even the one he describes extensively below.

and German excellently, and in the odd moments of her exciting occupations as a delegate, was conquering English.

I noticed that she seemed to take her position in the Soviet as a matter of course and her high standing among its speakers with unaffected modesty, but what did plainly seem to her strange was the position of women in the United States. She asked me many questions as to the reasons why all the women in America did not have the franchise, why they had it in some parts of the country and not in others, and was particularly struck with the fact that until the Congress then in session we had never had a woman in our national legislature. I believe that my efforts to explain this circumstance failed to convince her.

One of the other woman members of the Congress of Soviets was among its most impressive figures and abides in my memory always as the very image of Russia. She was neither young nor fair. She was tall, gaunt, gray haired, with furrowed face, extremely sad, and keen gray eyes. I used to see her sitting at her desk with her head resting on one hand, contemplating the proceedings with an expression of melancholy profound and tragic enough to move any beholder. I never saw her smile even when all the rest of the assembly was moved, as for instance by my peasant orator, to shouts of laughter, and although she took active interest in the proceedings it was in such a strangely detached way that I used to sit and wonder at her. She had been an exile and what she had endured must have burned out of her all capacity for mirth or any thoughts but sad thoughts.

Certainly the horror of it was reflected in her face. I thought I could see there the knout and the dripping dungeon, the long, weary journeyings, the long nights and frightful cold of the Arctic circle and the still worse things that wring the heart of every reader of the true story of such a martyr of human liberty as Maria Spiridonova, for instance.

It was while I was searching for Miss Spiridonova that I had a chance to see for myself how universal is the suspicion that generations of tyranny have bred in the Russian mind and at the same time how instinctive is the free masonry of common protection among the Russian women. I had secured from the committee in charge of the returned Siberian exiles what was supposed to be Miss Spiridonova's address in Petrograd. It was far over on the east side of the city, the third flat in a comfortable apartment house evidently occupied by the fairly well to do. A woman came in answer to our ring and as she opened the door and swept us with a keen glance I saw her face shut up like a pair of pincers. The first glimpse of her had shown a face of intelligence and ready wit. The next instant it had taken on the look of impenetrable dullness. My interpreter explained who I was and why I wanted to see her famous lodger. The woman listened as if she were making every effort to understand, but found it really too difficult for her poor struggling mind to grasp. Finally she said:

"Miss Spiridonova isn't here now."

"She lives here, does she not?"

"Oh, yes, she lives here, but she isn't in now."

"Do you know when she will be in?"

"No, she went out about 12 o'clock and did not say when she was coming back. But it will not be until very late," she added hastily, to head off any disposition we might have to wait. "She never comes in until very late. Midnight at least," she said impressively.

I left a note for her and said we would call again.

A day or two later I returned and had the same experience. But the next time I called the woman's husband was at home. He was a dentist, educated and having some knowledge of the world. When he was assured that I was not a spy nor any other emissary of evil and I did not want to assassinate Miss Spiridonova, he confided to me that she did not live at that address and never had lived there, but he told me where she did live and it was far away on the other side of the city, beyond the Neva, in what had been a school house but had now been commandeered for the use of the returned exiles, and where with five other women she occupied a room not much bigger than a closet.

She was the heroine and saint of the Revolution, she might have had anything she wanted, she might have luxury and ease, and she insisted upon sharing the lot of other exiles because she would not regard herself as any better or more deserving than they. And that I believe to be typical of the Russian woman Revolutionist.

The women's battalion, this far famed "Battalion of Death," had a history so perfectly Russian that it is not likely to be forgotten when much of the rest of these chronicles shall have slipped from men's minds.[10] Contrary to the world's belief on the subject, the purpose of the organization was not idle display nor even to shame the Russian slacker of the day. It was seriously and literally to go out and fight exactly as men fought. For women to fight was in Russia no novelty; long before the Battalion of Death was formed in Petrograd, thousands of women were fighting in the ranks of the Russian army. The first I saw of this phase of Russian life was at a railroad station on the Trans-Siberian. There had been some outbreaks of disorder at some of the stations and a command had been given that all of them should be guarded. At a station some distance east of Chita, two soldiers appeared on guard, one at each end of the little station building. One was a man and the other was a woman. She was dressed in full regimentals exactly like the man, she had her yellow hair twisted into a knot at the back of her head, just under the rim of her cap, and she paced to and fro with her bayoneted rifle on her shoulder in a manner so without self-consciousness that it was evident she was perfectly inured to the work. None of the natives, whether of the locality or upon the train, took the least notice of her, so that plainly she offered to them no novelty. It was the westerners that stared as at a marvel. A little farther along

---

[10] Shaming men into fighting was, in fact, a major reason that the Russian army and government created the several women's units. Their size was overall very small, as was their military role. Men soldiers generally disliked them and their purpose, i.e., to continue the war.

a woman was firing a railroad locomotive, but by this time the intrusion of women in fields of work hitherto held only by men had ceased to be new to us.[11]

On my way to and from the Embassy in Petrograd I used to pass the barracks of the warrior women and see them drilling. The spectacle was easy; they drilled in a little field at the rear of the barracks and quite open to the street. After watching them many times, it seemed to me they were as likely soldiers as any others I had seen. One thing that always impressed me was that they took themselves and their work with the utmost seriousness and with the same lack of self-consciousness I had remarked in the woman at the station. When they came into the field of battle they were to make good these high opinions of their soldierly attributes.

The commandant of the Petrograd battalion, Madame Botchkareva, I saw often.[12] She was a peasant, powerfully built, man-faced, grim, heavy-jawed, close-lipped. She again was a most serious soul (with such a face one could not expect her to be anything else) and had a mind like a parallelogram, innocent of the theatrical or the bizarre, and strange as it may seem, quite unaware that she had caused the nations to gossip about her. She was young, but already a veteran. She knew war, she had fought in the ranks. She had been married only a year or so when this war came and her young husband was called to the colors. Then he was killed in action, and she felt that her duty was to take his place in the ranks. She enlisted in a reserve regiment and had three months of training. Then she was added to a regiment in active service and went into battle.

All that any soldier knows of actual warfare she learned in bitter experience. She fought in the trenches with the water up to her waist, she charged with the rest of the line, she faced the machine-guns, and stood steady under the shrapnel. She was wounded and carried to the hospital; she recovered and went back to fight. Once all the regimental officers of her battalion were killed. There was no one to lead the troops. She sprang up and shouted to the men to follow her. They followed her and took two trenches.

She got the St. George's Cross and Medal for this, the highest decoration in the Russian army. In her next battle a machine-gunner was killed close by, and she arose voluntarily and took his place and got another St. George and Medal. Only four

---

[11] The woman soldier he describes probably was actually a railroad guard who had acquired such a uniform at a time when clothing was scarce. Women did indeed take over such guard roles because of the shortage of men caused by the war. There were women soldiers, but probably not in this place and duty.

[12] Botchkareva was indeed a remarkable example of a woman soldier. She had joined the tsarist army during the war, one of a few women who did so. Then, in 1917, she led the effort to form women's units and became a major 1917 political figure—as well as a figure in women's history. Note that I have left her name as he spells it, as do many others, with the letter "t." The modern spelling would be Bochkareva.

hundred of her regiment were left alive after that action; it was no common-place skirmish.

The survivors were reformed and sent to the Austrian front. In the first clash there she was wounded in the arm and shot through the body. That meant for her six months in the hospital. When she returned, it was with a captain's commission and another St. George and Medal. The next engagement in which she fought proved to be again a fierce conflict. The Austrians charged six times, and every time she led the counter charge that drove them back; her soldiers, seeing her uninjured, said she had a charmed life and wanted to fight again under her orders.

Her second in command of the Battalion of Death was the daughter of a Russian admiral, eighteen years old, convent-bred, and reared in luxury. While she was in the training-camp she slept on a board, dug trenches, ate the daily fare of the common soldier, and drilled with a rifle six hours a day. More than one of her companions came from the once so-called "noble" families; but the majority were of the workers, peasants like their commander, or the wives or daughters of Petrograd artisans.

Nearly all the women recruits voluntarily clipped their hair close to their skulls, the Russian soldier's favorite fashion. They wore the Russian soldier's ordinary uniform, belted tunic, trousers, high black boots. The first time I saw one she stalked thus garbed into a street-car. I looked at her with eyes of inattention; there were twenty other soldiers in that car attired exactly like her. Then my interpreter nudged me, and I looked again and made out that this was one of the Battalion of Death. The other passengers seemed to discover the fact about the same time. What most struck me was that everybody treated her with a gentle respect. There were many young men and young women on that car, but none of them laughed or gibed or commented. I wondered what would happen if this girl had stepped in the like circumstances into a street-car in America. Wondered? Nay, recalling certain scenes on the New York subway at night, I thought I knew.

On the following night I was in a restaurant, and four of them entered quietly and took seats. The other diners glanced up with curious interest, but nobody stared, nobody laughed, nobody favored us with hee-haw remarks.

The great square in front of St. Isaac's Cathedral was an impressive spectacle the day the women soldiers started for the trenches. The excellent Archbishop Platon of Petrograd, friend of America and friend of democracy, officiated at the solemn ceremony with which the Russian Church blesses the arms of those that go to war. The women marched into the square in smart, soldierly fashion; yet no one had reason to think they were on dress parade or viewed their task flippantly.

As to that you can judge better with some extracts from the address they issued to the country just before they left for the front:

"Russian Women!

"Our Mothers and Sisters!

"We write these lines with the blood of our hearts. Listen to us. Go with us in the name of your fallen heroes, dear to your memory.

"You, the valiant warriors, our soldiers of free Russia, you who have retained the sense of honor, of shame, of courage in your hearts, we turn to you. When will you raise your powerful voice and silence forever the cowardly lips of shameful Russian jackals dressed in soldiers' uniforms? Or are you waiting for the time when we shall be unable to distinguish between you and these traitors, when we shall be forced to look upon all soldiers with contempt? . . .

"We also turn to you, soldiers, cowards and traitors, who like Judas are selling Russia for thirty pieces of silver, bartering the sweat of your fathers and the bread of your children to the Germans.

"Soon, very soon, you will prefer to face ten German bayonets rather than one Russian tigress! We pour our maledictions upon you!"

But there were causes at work too deep to be reached by maledictions. A nation weary of a war it did not understand, and in which it had no interest, could not be made to fight by screaming proclamations. After so much gallant preparations in the lime light the finish of the story of the Battalion of Death was inglorious. It went to the front, it held some trenches, it was reported in one action to have fought bravely, to have taken some prisoners and lost some, and then came the Bolshevik upheaval of November, 1917, and all was over for the Battalion of Death. It was Russian. Being Russian it said as all other Russians said, "What's the use? These people are determined to do this kind of thing and they will do it anyway," and like the rest of Russia it sat down patiently to wait. "Nichy vo"—"it does not matter"—the characteristic Russian fatalism, had its perfect work. After all the drilling and the blessing, the clipping of fair locks and the donning of soldiers' attire, the result was no more than a share in the general collapse of the strength of Russia. At least it was so for the time being. Possibly the future may have another story to tell.

Chapter VII
The Peasant

Let a man have so much as an average gift of imagination, and let him come of a sudden and for the first time upon a typical Russian village, and though he be as optimistic as the lark the heart is likely to sink within him; all the more if the weather be gray.

Drearier place of habitation, he will say, is not known to man; even an American prairie town of forty years ago was not more dismal. A jumble of ancient roofs, partly in disrepair; a jumble of unpainted, uncompromising timber huts, gone gray like the sky; barn and dwelling, outhouse and toolhouse, askew along a lane of quag*mires* and deep, ancient ruts; superfluous indications of unkempt barnyard offending three senses; and over all an air that strikes the Westerner like a blow in the face, an air of seeming unthrift and neglect; that is his first impression and sometimes his last.

Hence, the average traveler from the West, being told that 75 per cent of Russia is peasant and nearly all of peasant Russia lives much like this, gives up in despair. Build a nation of such materials in such conditions? You might as well go build cathedrals of rushes!

But of course to the rigid Western sense everything in Russia is so wrong and so upside down that it should be read from right to left like Hebrew text. Poor looks the village, gloomy, forlorn and as without hope; yet it contains the very heart of Russia; it is the ceaseless dynamo of Russian political activity, it made the Revolution possible; those that saw closely the stages of the Revolution always believed it would make the Republic and make it great.

Everything in Russia comes home at last to the peasant; all must depend upon him. In 1860 he was a slave [serf] that owned not so much as his own hard and toiling hands.[1] The year 1917 beheld him in the seats of the mighty, shaping destiny, not only for his own country but for ours and all others. The fantastic whirligig of this our human existence may show some other upending like this, but surely on no such scale. I should think it one of the most stupendous things that ever happened. From

---

[1] They were not "slaves." Russia had a long history of distinguishing between slaves, who had no rights, and serfs, who did, and some other categories. Slavery was long gone by 1917, but like many foreigners he confused the two. Serfs were given approximately half the land and legal freedom from serf owners in 1861. Throughout he frequently uses "slavery" for serfdom. I sometimes insert an interpolation after "slavery" to remind readers of that, but often I leave his usage alone.

nothing to all in all went the peasant, almost in the turn of a hand. Other Russians might furnish much noise and hot-air currents, might parade with horrible banners and rattle conservatism with many threats. This Russian alone had power to decide between Bolshevik and Menshevik, wild-eyed and sane, frantic and reasonable; and what he said was in effect law.

He was greater than the Tsar ever was; he was not in the old phrase, "tempered by assassination," nor restrained by anything else.

He voted. He was the vast majority. He was the boss. And he lived in a down-at-the-heel village, where you would think gray tones and dreariness would beat Life flat, but where in spite of all he had learned practical wisdom of that same Life and been tutored in strange ways up to the job Fate had now laid upon him.[2]

In America there was a settled conviction that democracy was thrust suddenly upon Russia, that she had never heard of it before, that she was not at all prepared for it (as we were, for instance) and that hence democracy in Russia would prove impossible until, after a long period of tutelage, the people should have been raised to somewhere near our own high plane of development.

This was a grand belief and full of comfort. It absolved us from active interest in the Russian struggle or the least support of it, and enabled us with a sweet content to go back to our balance sheets, our automobiles and our golf links. Since Russia was unfit for democracy anyway, why bother about her?

Yet the historian will have it to observe that the idea of democracy as any novelty to the Russians was merely preposterous. If they were not fitted for it neither were we nor any other people on earth, and mankind went all wrong when it began to throw overboard its kings.

By faith and practice the Russians were among the most democratic of peoples and instead of being thumb-hand novices about democracy they had had much training in it.

Where? In that same ugly village. It had educated a Russia that was without books and almost without schools or a public press. It had taken the place of newspapers and telegraph. It had scattered information and broadened the general mind. To people that could not read it had taught the rudiments of human knowledge. And above everything else, it had stirred in them their innate love of liberty and made democracy more than a creed or a languid, remote and semi-fluid faith as often with us. Seemingly, it had made democracy in them a passion.

And again we ought to be slow to look down upon the dismal Russian village, because in respect to the future of the race and the actualities of life the Russian village might very well look down upon the American farmhouse.

---

[2] He, as many others, idealized the peasantry and its huge majority in numbers. Turning that majority into a functional national power was a serious problem, however, although he and many others of the time believed it was just around the corner. The capitalization of "Life" and "Fate" reflected his giving them special meaning.

Either as an invention or an instrument of civilization, the village is immeasurably the superior of the farmhouses.[3] Society in the village may not be such as would stir enthusiasm in Park Lane and upper Fifth Avenue, but it is at least society. Men and women meet and exchange ideas, rub mind against mind, divide information, share and share alike, put into a common fund whatever wit may be in fifty minds, whatever of life may have been seen by a hundred eyes, whatever may have been experienced by fifty souls.

In the remote farmhouse, shut off from the world of men, marooned on a prairie island, single couples or single families lose all faculty for united effort and, driven in upon themselves, become the most hopeless individualists on earth. The thing works out as might be expected. Here, for instance, is this great cooperative movement that in the last twenty years has remade life for millions in Europe. Those immense and highly successful cooperative societies of Belgium (before she was bludgeoned), France, Italy, Switzerland, Serbia, have cheapened the cost of living and raised its standard until they have become among the greatest benefactors of the race. But observe that while in Russia cooperation has been a conspicuous success, in America, after a thousand well-meant attempts and many ingenious devices, it remains to a certain extent a failure. Russians, graduates of the village scheme of life, naturally cooperate; Americans, graduates of the farmhouse scheme of life, naturally do not. Every man for himself—it is the sure reflex of solitary living and the farmhouse.

Or, to take another illustration, it might be profitable to consider how far the United States, before the war, lagged behind the rest of the world in the development of communal enterprises and the communal spirit that, until scattered by the Iron Fist, was beginning to show a new era in the affairs of men.

In Russia there are no solitary farmhouses. The farmers always live in villages. An Anglo-Saxon seems to like to get away from his fellows; the Russian demands their company. As a rule, the land the Russian farmer tills lies close beside the village where he lives, but near or far, he goes forth to his day's work from his village home and returns thither when the day's work is done.

Amusement in that village, the interchange with his neighbors of ideas and experiences, the gossip and chatter, the disputes and arguments, may not be very exciting, but they have been something for him to look forward to all day, and enough, when they come, to prod his mind out of the ruts of drudgery and sometimes to spur it into the health of continued activity.

Where the system of communal land ownership prevails in Russia the peasant does not own the land he tills because all the land there belongs to the community of which he is a member, but he may own the house in which he lives, the tools with which he works, the horses, cows and chickens in his barnyard. He shelters his live-

---

[3] Here he contrasts the Russian rural village, where the population lived and then went off to work the land around it, with the American farm system, where most people lived on their own separate farmland. The Russian system fit into his socialist ideology.

stock unpleasantly near to his own place of abiding, but that is all one to him. He is used to it, as his forbears were before him. Yet he is not a dirty person, as doubtless you have been led to believe; no more dirty than he is stupid. Customs differ greatly in different parts of the country, but you often find in Russia the village bathhouse as much of an institution as the village church or shrine and more regularly visited, while some of the peasants' homes have their own bathing apparatus. Apparatus is the apt word, for the bath is always of steam; that is what a bath means to a Russian. He gets upon a shelf in a room dense with hot steam and there sweats and is rubbed with twigs and scrubbed in hot water and in cold, and goes home clean and content maybe for Sunday, for Saturday is a favorite bathing occasion.

In the old days he used frequently to mark the day, religious or festal, by getting drunk on it—there is no doubt of that, although he was never so bad as he was painted. But in 1917 all that had been changed with the rest. Prohibition came easily in Russia; the Government had a monopoly of the rum trade and cut it off with one blow of the ax by going out of the business.[4] No doubt there was some illicit distilling at the time of our visit but it could not be very extensive, because I circulated among all kinds of people and saw only two men under the influence of liquor. After all, are there any fixed habits or customs? Vodka was supposed to be indispensable to the average Russian, yet in a day it was swept away from him and he did not revolt. Today he doesn't care; he seems to have forgotten all about it; and no matter what else may happen in Russia it seems a safe prediction that vodka will never be voted back. The women are against it, and unless an exterior power totally destroys the new democracy in Russia the women will vote. That is one weighty consideration. But even if there were only male suffrage I doubt that it would ever be possible to arouse any enthusiasm for the return of the rum fiend. He seems to have gone into a permanent exile.[5]

When I was there the people were not drinking beer in the place of vodka, nor yet wine, perfumery, wood alcohol, varnish nor any other of the substitutes that it was predicted of the wise men they would fly to. There is no native wine except some of high price and exquisite quality that is made in the Crimea, and as for beer, that was bowled out with the rum fiend. In place of these the favorite drink is *kvass*, a beverage made from rye bread and often extremely good. It looks something like light beer but usually is without alcohol. There is no punch in *kvass*, but a man does not go home and beat up his family after he has been drinking it; that is one compensation. Of course you can find all manner of fault with the peasant if you wish to; there is material enough. It is true that he is not eager for fresh air. The temperature in winter may sink

---

[4] Alcohol prohibition was ordered in 1914 at the outbreak of the war in order to facilitate the mobilization of soldiers, and then continued on throughout the war. Heavy drinking continued, however. If, in 1917, he only saw two drunks, that reflects that he, like most visitors, was kept away from them.

[5] He was optimistic, but completely wrong here.

as low as 60° or 70° below zero and he has no yearning for much of it. Every window in his log house is double; the cracks all around it are conscientiously caulked with a vegetable fiber like wool. In some windows is a small hinged pane that can be opened, but seldom is; except for this the thing is air-tight. The logs in the walls are trimmed down much closer than in any log house we know, and the surfaces are trimmed until they seem to fit perfectly, but even this bare chance of a crack is caulked and plastered. The door is heavy, tightly fitted and seldom opened. If a breath of fresh air gets into that house it must steal in as an enemy and take the family unaware.

This close atmosphere is overheated with a huge brick oven on the top of which sleep the old people and the children. Sometimes the temperature stands at 80° or more; 75° is common. You would think they would all die of colds or tuberculosis, but they do not; there seems to be a link out of the fresh-air theory when it comes to Russia. Tuberculosis is worse in many a country where ventilation is much farther advanced, and while infant mortality is shockingly high and the death-rate in Petrograd greater than in London, the peasant's average of health, except in one respect, may be called good.

The exception belongs to the old system and helps to indict it in a way I shall speak of later. Like the generality of Russian people, the peasant was susceptible to diseases of nervous origin. These, great doctors found, were the products of worry, care and depression, and in turn, these black demons flocked in the shadow of the terror that lay across the land.[6]

The obvious reason why, even in the old days, the peasant, whether ill or well, was of sturdy frame, was that for centuries his tribe had been well nourished. In spite of the fact that they have little meat and a narrowly limited dietary otherwise, Russian countrymen seem to live rather well and, considering the poor materials they have, to be the world's premium cooks. They can take a handful of cabbage or potatoes or something and make soups that are dreams of delight; of their simplest dishes they will make something appetizing and attractive.

I have gone aside to these remarks because are we so liberal of our pity of the poor, half-starved Russian when as a matter of fact he is typically of physical might and ruddy vitality. Also because it pertains, after all, to my subject. Social progress demands full stomachs, and I was convinced that the outlook in Russia would not be half so good if the people were not so full-blooded.[7]

We can never rid ourselves of the notion that an illiterate person must necessarily be both dull and uninformed. Yet if we were to teach to an illiterate all the contents

---

[6] This idea was widespread in and about Russia at the time.

[7] His image here was quite off, but probably reflected what he was told there, and perhaps the villages he visited were carefully selected to make a good impression. Many Russians fit his description, but large portions suffered from hunger and ill health. Russia underwent major famines at various times, including in the late nineteenth century. Both the February and October Revolutions arose in part out of food shortages.

of any book he would know as much about it as an average reader, and might easily make a better use of it. The Russian villagers were often illiterate; they seldom saw a newspaper and until recent years seldom had a school; but they sensed something of what was going on in the world and had even some outlines of rudimentary knowledge, because the village was school and newspaper.

The villages were so near together that news and information went swiftly and easily from one to another. Say a traveler arrived at Polosk at eight o'clock bearing news that a great fire had destroyed San Francisco. By nine o'clock someone would slip over to Tomolosk, and then someone from Tomolosk would pass it along to Levolf, and by nightfall all the villages in the valley would have heard of the disaster and the tongues would be clacking like mill-wheels.

It might not be wholly accurate information, but it would contain the germs of knowledge and thought; and ceaseless discussion of it sharpened the wits and schooled the tongue.

Similarly about other things. Suppose a school to be opened in one of the larger villages. More pupils drank at its fountains than could ever sit within its walls, I can assure you.

The village taught the people to talk, which is the Russian national game. Russians are the master talkers of the world. The vocabulary of the average Russian peasant is three times as large as the vocabulary of the average toiler of any other nation, and about twice as large and four times as effective as the vocabulary of the average member of Congress. The Russian's fluency and readiness of speech are amazing; often he can talk on for hours without hesitating for a word or struggling overhard to get his ideas into clothes to fit them.[8]

He learned how in the village.

The village, also, is responsible for the extraordinary development of peasant industries, at the produce of which all visitors stand amazed.

Russian winters have long nights, short hours of daylight and grim, menacing skies. Men seem driven together in such conditions and compelled to some kind of indoor work for ease of mind.[9] A group of peasants sits in a row doing two things, gabbling and wood-carving. The first man cuts from the block a straight piece of wood two inches wide, an inch and a half thick, six inches long, and passes it thus to Number 2.

Number 2 cuts in the sides of it indentations half an inch deep, three inches long, and passes it thus to Number 3.

Number 3 cuts the edges round and makes a handle and passes it thus to Number 4.

---

[8] Again, a romantic view of the villages.

[9] And, more importantly, to make a living.

THE PEASANT

Number 4 hollows out one side near the end and rounds off the other and passes it thus to Number 5.

Number 5 covers it with varnish and lays it away to dry.

It is a wooden spoon.

Meantime, as the work of the hands is more or less mechanical, it interferes nothing with the national game, and conversation pours through that place in a ceaseless tide. Yet you are not to infer that in the old days it was breezy conversation nor even cheerful, always. The Russian does not easily get far from his native melancholy. And you are not to suppose that if then the talk flowed amply the talkers ever forgot the fear that lay on all hearts or that they touched upon the things forbidden. There were spies in every village as in every city, and from every doorway the road to Siberia could be easily seen, the road of blood and tears.

The peasant women are busy, too. They take a handful of wool and spin it into a shawl as light as gossamer, glistening like snow and so soft one can put it into a teacup and take it out unwrinkled.

They make amazing things out of lace. I never mastered the names of these devices, but the feminine world seems to be always moved at the sight of them to rhapsodical delight, which I assume to be sufficient evidence of their worth.

They take wheat straws, these peasants, and color them and then weave them into dainty baskets and jewel-cases widely celebrated for artistic design and color scheme.[10]

They take the inner bark of the white birch and make of it stout valises, suit-cases and traveling bags.

They become expert metal workers and turn out gewgaws like belt buckles and that sort of thing.

They make shoes from bark.

They make ingenious toys and paint them handsomely.

They can carve in wood almost anything that was ever carved in it and weave in wool almost anything that ever was woven.

Many of them reveal a natural talent for painting, and without instruction paint native landscapes and village scenes.

They can sing, sometimes like angels and sometimes not, but always well, and they can dance. Russian church music, of course, far excels all other music of the kind; everybody knows that; and the folksongs seem almost as remarkable. When it comes to dancing, the Russian peasant dance seems to merit the praise it gets because it often has humor and a story as well as grace and rhythm.

After one has contemplated the statistics of that development of Russian cooperation of which I have spoken, and has grasped the fact that most of it is of peasant or-

---

[10] Russian villages, especially in the northern areas, spent the winter opening up the rivers and making items that could be shipped to cities come spring.

igin and direction, the menace of peasant ignorance and incompetence seems to have less substance. So soon as the Revolution had set free the minds and souls of men, cooperation, which had always been strong in Russia, went forward with new speed. On July 1, 1914, there were in Russia 30,000 local cooperative societies of all kinds; by July 1, 1917, those had grown to 50,000, with an estimated membership of close to 15,000,000. Suppose each member to represent a household, which is a fair estimate, and each Russian household to have the average number of persons that prevails in other countries, which is certainly not too much to allow, nearly one-half of the total population of Russia was participating in the benefits of cooperation at a time when it was all but impossible to make a cooperative society in America survive for a year.[11]

There are in Russia 4,000 artels, or cooperative societies of workingmen, formed to handle the products of the domiciliary industries.

There are about 6,000 farmers' cooperative societies whose functions are to buy the things farmers need and sell the farmers' produce on a cooperative basis.

There are more than 20,000 Consumers' Purchasing societies, operating stores mostly in villages, although, in Moscow there is one such society that has 65,000 members. These organizations began to be formidable only after the unsuccessful Revolution of 1905, when the peasants were stirred by their defeat to make unusual efforts to improve their condition and to enlarge their resources.

There are about 16,000 cooperative Savings, Loan and Credit Associations. Of these the Credit Associations among the peasants have done a most useful work and grown far beyond the original lines of their endeavors. They now buy all kinds of machinery and supplies to sell to their members on the instalment plan, lend money to their members to handle the crops, assist in marketing products and act as business agents and functionaries.

There is in Siberia one Union of Creameries Associations that controls on a cooperative basis the products of more than 1500 creameries and operates 1050 stores for the benefit of its members.

There is another in Eastern Siberia that has 233 local associations in its organization and in 1917 did a business of 150,000,000 rubles, equivalent in ordinary times to $75,000,000. There are two other similar associations in Siberia almost as large. Before the war they maintained a sales office so far away as London.

The Moscow Union of Consumers' Societies, an organization for wholesale supplies, had in 1898 67 local societies as its members. In 1915 these had increased to 1,700 and in 1917 to 2,500. It operates flour mills, tobacco factories, fish salting establishments, shoe factories and other enterprises.

The cooperative societies of Moscow maintain a bank that began in 1912 with a capital of 1,000,000 rubles and has now a capital of 10,000,000 rubles and depos-

---

[11] He was fascinated with the cooperatives, which had a following among socialists such as himself. They were widespread, and most socialists saw in them evidence of a Russian peasant inclination toward socialism.

its and assets of 80,000,000. It did a business in 1917 of 3,000,000,000 rubles. In 1917 this bank contracted for 125,000 harvesting machines and 18,000 tons of binder twine.

The cooperative societies are generally organized into district associations and these into national associations. Throughout all these vast and complicated associations is displayed an extraordinary talent for coordinated effort and union, for no other country in the world makes in cooperation relatively as good a showing. And yet I have heard a Senator of the United States declare that the Russians have so little capacity for organized effort that it is useless to expect they can ever make a nation of themselves.

For the most part these gigantic distributing machines have been built primarily out of the intelligence and persistence of the peasant. The facts about them must certainly reveal him in a light very different from any in which we have ever been accustomed to see him.

Yet the other notions about typical peasant life, of which I spoke in the first chapter, are all but universal and for this generation probably immovable. Attempts to change them have even been resented, as if they were some form of religion. It would seem that a little philosophical reflection would show to almost anyone that changes in the peasant's situation had worked great changes in his activities and influence. For instance, when slavery [serfdom] existed in Russia it was gross, cruel, primitive, and as frank as a pair of leg-irons. So many cattle, so many serfs, so many swine, was the owner's inventory, viewing all alike and selling one as indifferently as another. Close over the serf's bent back hung the whip, and few fields were tilled or roads made except to the tune of its lashings. That was but sixty years ago. The first generation of freedom bore still the heavy stamp of all this accursed system and had to bear it; not with one leap could freedmen come to the full stature of the free; and while we do not know it, the peasant that we cling to as the type is nothing but the first rebound from slavery [serfdom].

It was the time when Russian literature burst upon the world in its awe-compelling power and it carried with it this accepted and still popular style of peasant portraiture.

But the present generation is different. Even before the Revolution, the peasants we had always thought so ignorant and stupid were publishing peasants' newspapers filled with clever writing, manifesting the first signs of a huge cultural revolt and making some exceedingly good poetry. And of course, at the sound of the Revolution, all this burst forth without restraint and he must be a dull observer that cannot see a new era.

It is still the fashion in this country, and probably will long be so, to make much of the illiteracy of the Russian people. After a time I gathered a shrewd impression that if the Russians had other ideas about an ideal social state their reported illiteracy would have been far less conspicuous. Pleas for social justice can be easily discounted if they can be assumed to come from some appalling slough of ignorance and illiteracy. As to the ignorance, that is a term indefinite and relative. Ignorance of book lore is great and widespread. Lack of information common in other countries is also very extensive and a great evil. These things could not be otherwise; reflect upon the immensity of the country, the lack of an adequate railroad system, the *miry* roads; reflect upon the system of popular education, so new and ill-established. I would not regard these terrible handicaps lightly. But the point I make is that considering all his burdensome disadvantages the intelligence of the typical peasant is remarkable and may justly give us hope and confidence; for his mind is alert and his capacity proven.

As to the actual present-day conditions of illiteracy, nobody knows, but while we still hold to the traditional 80 per cent of illiteracy for all Russia it is plain enough that this is absurd. Peasant newspapers are not published for illiterates, which is but one of the many facts that show the vast changes of the last fifteen years. Almost every considerable village has come to have its school. Education, which used to be the exclusive right of the few, is on the way to be universal if Russian democracy is allowed to work out its own destiny.[12]

This chapter of history might well be called The Story of Foolish Rulers that Thought they Could Stop Progress, because in the most wonderful way the things the old rotten Government thought would surely perpetuate the old system were the things that pulled it down. The Revolution of 1905, for instance: that was suppressed (on the Kaiser's advice) with an iron will and the most horrible cruelty, that it might be a memorable and lasting example to all, but it helped tremendously to force the Government's hand about education, and education turned out to be autocracy's deadliest foe. Even the dull, feeble-minded, cruelty loving Tsar is said to have been impressed, after 1905, with the idea that the old policy of keeping the people in ignorance would have to be shifted, and when he did that he cut the mainstay of his throne.

Today any visitor can see that Russian illiteracy, although still far too great, is no longer overwhelming, as it once was. In proportion to the population, more daily newspapers are published in Petrograd, for example, than in any other city in the world. Some of the journals of Petrograd, Moscow and Odessa have huge circulations, one of those in Moscow ranking within the first ten of newspapers everywhere. Newspaper reading is visibly a common habit. As I have pointed out before, there is the significant evidence of the National representing them, contained among its 830 delegates only twenty illiterates. Once so many railroad men were unable to read that the freight-cars carried on their sides pictorial instructions for coupling. Recently no such illustrations have been needed. Finally, most of the illiterates of this day are thirty-five years old or more. The younger element generally can read.

---

[12] Following the Great Reforms of 1861 and then industrialization, literacy had picked up significantly by his time.

The village organization was often a vehicle for Revolutionary propaganda and the Revolutionary propaganda taught the peasant many things besides Revolution. If the whole story could be written as it really happened, it would leave all fiction in the world cold for interest. Every hour of a propagandist's life throbbed with fierce excitement; he was bent upon outwitting and outmaneuvering the spies that surrounded him, but he knew that any moment they might break through upon him and hurl him to the horrible living death of exile. As he stealthily spread his doctrine, he wove into it the outlines of the long, upward struggle of the human cause. The story went slowly from mouth to mouth, from village to village, just as the news of the San Francisco fire spread, perhaps; but it went until a large part of the mass had a smattering of it and therein had also the germs of education.

Meantime the Government, with all its illimitable power and ruthless cruelty, stood by to prevent this work. It surrounded Russia with a wall to keep out the literature it feared, and lo! the substance of that literature seeped under or floated over or crept through. One of the historic episodes it was especially resolved to bar from the country was the story of the American Revolution. All Revolutions looked bad to the dull, blundering Government, but for sufficient reasons this looked the worst. It allowed John Fiske's[13] other historical writings to be translated and circulated, but a strict ban was on his account of our Revolution. Yet the story went by the village-to-village telegraph, and millions of peasants that could not read knew the substance of the American struggle and honored the name of George Washington. The truth seems to be that there is no stopping of these things; the whole force of the great Russian Government was put forth to check democracy, and democracy grew and spread and sprang up in that Government's very face.

In 1917, the dream of the Russian Republic that was to be, included education free, universal, compulsory. Also it was to be so arranged that the poorest should have as much chance at it, in even its highest forms, as the wealthy have now. Education bulwarks democracy and democracy advances education, and these were, after all, the first ripened fruits of the iron oppression that the Kaiser so much commended to his friend the Tsar. What was the use?

When a nation starts upon the road to freedom, even the worst conditions serve only in the end to help it along. Slavery [serfdom], for instance. Slavery could not have endured in Russia more than in any other country. And yet slavery should never have been abolished if the autocratic form of government was to live, because the blow that felled Russian slavery dug the burying-place of Russian monarchy.

Thus: At the time of the emancipation vast areas of land were in the possession of the State which is to say, of the Tsar. Some of this was tilled, and it seems strange now to think that it was tilled by slaves [serfs] that the State owned; but the greater

---

[13] Fiske was a major American historian and author in the second half of the nineteenth century.

part was unproductive and so remains to this day. Outside of the State lands, agricultural Russia was in the hands of the nobles and great landowners, who were also the serf-owners and often held huge estates.

When the Government abolished slavery [serfdom] in 1861, it was driven without any will of its own to a singular act of justice. Even to its limited intelligence the fact was clear enough that to set all these millions of slaves suddenly free and to provide them with no means of livelihood would pull down a great disaster. It therefore provided that the national treasury should advance to them enough money to buy the land they had formerly tilled as serfs, repayment to be made on easy terms in forty-nine years. The landlords were brought to look complacently upon this scheme by an intricate system of compensations not necessary to be described here.

In the case of serfs that had been held by the State, grants were made from the State lands.

The Romanovs didn't know it, but they were signing themselves out of their jobs when they adopted such a reform. It begot the village *mir* in its modern shape and the village *mir* begot the Russian Republic, while Citizen Nicholas Romanoff from the windows of an indifferent house at Tobolsk looked out upon a dreary section of the country he used to rule.

Mir means "world" or "union." The village *mir* means that the affairs of that village are its world, which is true and a good term. The *mir* is an old institution in Russia, but since the rise of absolutism and the suppression of the ancient freedom it had become largely nominal. The reform measures now revived it and made it a thing of might.

In delivering the land to the late serfs the plan followed was that all the serfs that had belonged to one master should receive in common all of the land they had tilled and constitute one community, or *mir*. In most cases the village and all the land around it had been owned by one nobleman or seigneur. The new arrangement made such a village of potential and actual democracy.

It had land to control and business to transact.

The land must be allotted and re-allotted among the peasant proprietors, all of whom, as I have said, lived in the village and went out to till the fields. Some of the crops—as hay, for instance—were sometimes harvested, handled and marketed on the common account. The security of the village must be provided for and its affairs regulated by some new authority, now that the noble or seigneur had nothing to do with it.

Therefore each village had its assembly, in which all of the peasants took part and everything was decided by majority vote.

In other words, the Romanoffs lay awake nights to think how they could keep out the democratic camel and then got up in their sleep and seized the patient creature by the neck and ears and dragged him all the way into the tent.

Exactly that, because here was as good a school of practical democracy as ever was invented and there was hardly an hour when it was not at work.

Each village elected a village elder, or mayor, who represented the community in its dealings with the national Government, collected the taxes and looked after the local improvements. Taxes were assessed on the village in a lump sum and split among the peasant proprietors by the assembly. In respect to all local affairs it was the active authority. The villagers met and discussed their problems with much freedom so long as they breathed nothing of disloyalty or revolt, and decided each issue by a majority vote. It was plainly a good way to decide things. But the problems of the nation were not discussed and decided in any such way. They were decided by a half-witted person sitting upon a throne in Petrograd and chiefly distinguished for a facility in pulling his mustache and listening to a depraved impostor that called himself a monk and was none.[14]

Such a condition could no more last than tow [flax or hemp] could last in the burning pit. It was not in nature, it was impossible. If the people were going to rule about their local affairs they were some day going to rule no less about their national affairs. And that is exactly what happened.

The leaven of democracy brought in by the revived and freshened *mir* was pushed along about the same time by the revival of another old institution, the assembly of the *volost*, or canton. The village assemblies elected delegates to the cantonal assembly.

Three years later, 1864, the same idea was farther advanced when the *zemstvo*[15] was created. One business of the *zemstvo* was to foster the interests of agriculture; another, legally, was to tamper with the tax schedules. After it had gone on some years merrily loading the taxes upon the peasants and slipping them from the shoulders of the wealthy, a different order of mind appeared in it, a mind with wit enough to perceive that you could not rob the producers forever without impoverishing the nation and everybody in it. Prince Lvov, for some months prime minister of the Provisional Government, was a good example of this type. He spent many years in *zemstvo* work and was long the head of the national union of *zemstvos*. He and his kind went early to the task of making the *zemstvo* an institution that should develop the interests of all the people alike.

Under this leadership, the *zemstvo* introduced new methods in peasant agriculture and marketing. It greatly developed the peasants' industries I have spoken of. It supported cooperation. It opened stores in many places for the sale of peasants' products. It started their exports. It encouraged the native skill and artistic sense and

---

[14] He is referring here to Rasputin.

[15] *Zemstvo* was a local government institution created by Alexander II in 1864 as part of the Great Reforms. Authority and representation varied over time, but they played an important and hopeful role regarding Russia's future.

was on the way greatly to improve and brighten every feature of peasant life when the blight of war blew upon it.

The union of *zemstvos*, a body whose growing power and rapidly expanding field even the coldblooded autocracy was forced to acknowledge, turned its attention to the war and the condition of the troops, and was able to bring about substantial improvements. It maintained hospitals, collected and forwarded hospital stores and attempted relief for the monotony of soldiers' lives when troops are held in reserve, as were most of the Russians.

The remade and freshened *mir* did more than to drive into people's heads the rudiments of democratic faith; it taught them the use of it. The delegates to the national soviets that with their parliamentary skill and facile eloquence so astonished Western visitors were graduates of the *mir*. It taught them how public business may be transacted and made discussion as familiar to them as the handles of their plows. Nothing is more democratic anywhere; not even the New England town meeting, which the *mir* much resembles.

But against the suggestion of the Russian peasant as a competent soldier of democracy there rises always that picture of the old typical peasant of our esteemed fiction, singing with unction "God Save the Tsar" and doing reverence before a picture of the "Little Father." How touching that used to be—to those of us that have a strong slant of snobbery still in the blood! Those dear, simple-minded peasants, so sweetly loyal to their emperor!

All this we may now well forget, or retain as no more than the artistry and literary embroidery of another generation. The Russian peasant used to fall on his knees before the Tsar and very likely have on his walls an ikon of that distinguished mustache grower, but it was because he knew the police spy was watching him and Siberia loomed in the background.

In 1917 the Tsar, as you may surmise from the adventures of his private car, would have good reason to tremble if ever he fell into the hands of those dear peasants, and as for having him on their backs again, they would as soon have the devil.

Prince Paul Troubetskoy[16] was perfectly right when he perpetrated upon the old regime the stupendous irony of all sculpture in that great statue he made of Tsar Alexander the Third. It stands in the square before the principal railroad station and commands the wondering attention of every fresh beholder, for in all the wide world is nothing like it. The burly figure of the Tsar appears seated menacingly upon a huge, ungainly, bit-champing horse. The municipality employed Troubetskoy to create a work of art in honor of the dead ruler, and he made one that will not quickly pass from human memory. And after he made it and was safe in Paris he might have laughed so loudly that all the world should hear him.

---

[16] Trubetskoi was a member of an aristocratic family who had gained considerable fame as an artist and mostly was living abroad. His spelling of the name was common.

For he had deliberately pictured in his statue the big, coarse, brutal Tsar riding the Russian people, holding to his seat by the sheer force of the terror he created, and the great Russian people, ridden, but never consenting to be ridden. All the words of all the tongues of all mankind could not better express the exact situation.

When the sculptor's gigantic sarcasm dawned upon them, some Russians were for taking the statue down, and very likely that would have been its fate but for the Revolution. It will not come down now. It will stay where it is, the final memorial of a dark and monstrous era that has passed from the world like a hideous dream.

Chapter VIII
The Bolshevik

"In the next cage, ladies and gentlemen, you will find that singular beast, the fierce, fiery, man-eating Bolshevik. This ferocious creature goes to and fro upon the earth, seeking whom he may devour, and as he strides along upon his horrid errand the ground shakes beneath his tread, he breathes forth fire and brimstone, and all animate nature flees in terror from the appalling sight."

It was in some such manner as this, as a self-satisfied showman would introduce a rare novelty, that many newspaper correspondents in the fall of 1917 presented to the public this new terror of the nations, dwelling with manifest delight upon the strange and alarming name of the destroying monster. Bolshevik—Bolshevik! What is a Bolshevik? Nobody knew, but by the sound of it, something awful. When to this vague but disconcerting apparition was added the suggestion that the coming of the Bolshevik meant in some way ravin and ruin here as well as in Russia, it was no wonder that there began a furious assault upon him—with paper bullets.[1]

But to see the Bolshevik as he really was, to visit him in his own habitat, was to reduce these horrifying specters to the pleasant realm of whimsy. Instead of being an abnormal product, the Bolshevik was in Russia the most natural fruitage; no plant ever grew more naturally from any seed than he was processed from the old regime in Russia. Natural? Nay, he was inevitable. By no possibility could there be anywhere on this earth the conditions that existed in the old Russian system without sooner or later producing Bolsheviks. If the Russian Revolution had not disclosed them the lack would be a sign of ill-health; all persons that have any skill in national diagnosis would say there was something wrong.

Also, there was nothing in the fundamental objects of the Russian Bolsheviks that was in itself of evil impulse, although the newspapers easily induced almost all the American public to believe that there was. Every Revolution that amounts to anything sets free a vast swarm of theories and theorists. If it fails to have that result it fails to be a Revolution, because it fails then to have the basis of profound and genuine

---

[1] The Bolsheviks had just taken power when he wrote this. It appeared to many that a new, better era of human history had begun. The terrible things that went down in history had not, of course, happened yet.

feeling that alone can make a Revolution valuable or successful; and these theories must have their chance to be worked out or exhaust their impetus.

Readers of American history should have needed no instruction on this point; they should have remembered that we had eleven years of conflicting ideas before we settled down upon a Constitution—and one far from perfect at that. Lessons drawn from the French Revolution were equally pertinent.

But it quickly appeared that at the first hinted analogy with the French Revolution a part of the public leaped to the handy conclusion that the Bolshevik was a *sans culotte* and was about to begin a Reign of Terror.[2] This was all wrong: the Bolshevik was no *sans culotte* and nothing could have been farther from his cherished aims than a Reign of Terror. He was, in fact, the most interesting and important outgrowth of awakened Russia, he was a sign of the Russian mentality, exotic but genuine, he was for the time being the true word of Russian thought, he held for some months the fate of the world in his grasp, and it was deplorable that while there was ceaseless but all wasted assault upon him—as if he could be overturned in Russia by attacking him in Jonesville, Pennsylvania—there was almost no effort to understand him.

Yet this would have been no hard task. First of all, it was necessary to remember that he was a dreamer—a dreamer of pleasant, kindly, agreeable dreams that in another age of the earth's story may not be dreams at all but the corner stone of society. To the sincere but unreasoned conviction of the Bolshevik, the whole world was wrong but could easily be made right. All it needed was a little application of the Grand Rejuvenating Elixir, and he knew the formula for the mixture and was ready to apply it. Lay some of this on the world's hurt, was his notion, and see how quickly everything that is wrong will become right.[3]

There was, of course, nothing new about this kind of amiable obsessionist. At least once in every generation the woods have been full of him. There was nothing new in his absolute and almost matchless sincerity. If the dreamer were not sincere he could never win anybody to his dreams. But the fanatic usually has the world before him to be converted. What was peculiar about the Bolshevik was that he believed (for a time) the world, or the greater part of it, already converted to his dreams and needing only a signal to arise and make them a reality for all mankind. And for the post of herald of this gracious transformation, dawn-bringer to the peoples dwelling in darkness, he himself, the Bolshevik of Russia, was ordained. At twelve o'clock he would beat upon his bell in Petrograd. At one o'clock the proletariat in all countries would stand forth and declare the new order, and by sundown in all the world the old social structure would have been pulled down and a new one erected. Whereupon,

---

[2] An important radical phase of the French Revolution. Comparing the French and 1917 Russian revolutions was common at the time.

[3] This view was in fact held by most Russian revolutionaries of 1917, including the Bolsheviks. The more violent stages of the revolutionary era had not yet begun when he wrote.

sound the loud timbre! The race is freed, wars will be no more, racial and national lines are wiped out, no more dissension, no more strife, the lion and the lamb will do their long-advertised and justly-famous performance before applauding millions, and the world will live happy ever afterward, a band of brothers.

And what was to overthrow the existing social system? The torch and ax? Not at all. No violence. The proletariat of the world was to march once around the walls of Jericho blowing a tin horn, when down would go the walls, joy follow, and oppression vanish.

He meant it. He was in most sober earnest about it. The thing was so daylight-clear to him that he would never admit (because he could not conceive) that everybody else did not see it—except, of course, the small and unimportant capitalist class, and they blinded themselves to it because they were about to lose their privileges. All the rest of the world looked upon the matter exactly as the Bolshevik looked upon it; because, of course, there was no other possible way to look at it. All the world was really Bolshevik, but because of the tyranny and accursed oppression of the capitalist, dare not say so. Yet it would arise and cast off its yoke when the Bolshevik should give the word.

It was a sad disillusion that awaited these moon-struck dreamers. The world was in a state of war. How terrible is war! Let us end the war and then usher in everywhere the glad proletarian rule. So they invited all the warring nations to come to a peace conference and, when the nations failed to respond, they entered upon the fatal negotiations at Brest-Litovsk and awoke to find the claws of the German vulture in the heart of their new born Republic.[4]

From all this the Bolshevik might be inferred to be an ignorant man. That again would be error. He was often very well-informed—about everything except the world's attitude toward the hobby-horse that so gallantly and persistently he rode. When I was in Petrograd I passed many pleasant hours with typical Bolsheviks. Invariably I found them abounding in courtesy and well-equipped with culture and information, but once mounted upon the facile hobby-horse, flashing far away like the elfin rider that, to tell the truth, they considerably resembled.

For what was the new structure of society that at one o'clock the enlightened proletariat was to erect upon the ruins of the old, fallen to pieces at noon? So nearly as I could gather, it was based and projected much as follows:

1. In common with Mensheviks, Minimalists, Trudoviks, and practically everybody else in Russia, the Bolsheviks accepted the general outlines of the

---

[4] The Bolsheviks did indeed push to get a general, universal negotiated peace. That quickly failed, and the Bolsheviks gave in to the reality that the Allies would not join such an effort, and that any Russian government that tried to continue the war would lose popular support and probably collapse. They therefore turned to separate peace negotiations with Germany and its allies. Ironically, some Russian conservatives had turned toward a peace with Germany also.

Socialist philosophy. They believed that all wealth is created by labor and that labor is entitled to the wealth it creates. They believed, that is to say, in industrial democracy. They believed that to bring about industrial democracy, all industries should be owned by and operated for the benefit of the community.

2. But they went much farther than this by believing that these changes could be and should be wrought at once and that instantly there should be instituted likewise these essential principles:
    A. All men and women should work.
    B. All men and women that work should be organized into unions.
    C. Each union should have its central governing council.
    D. These central councils should constitute all the government there is in this world. No congresses, no presidents, no parliaments, no prime ministers, no cabinets, no legislatures, no governors, nothing but the councils of the unions.

With the utmost sincerity they could see nothing about these changes more difficult than the issuing of a proclamation or two.

But while part of the world bellowed laughter, part sneered and part raved at this program, the fact remained that it was a thing typically Russian and the strange, new force that had been let loose upon mankind had a kind of altruistic basis, after all, not half so amusing as it was fine and high. The Bolshevik himself was not a Bolshevik because he wanted advantages on his own account. Even when the Bolshevik coup of October, 1917, came and so many things were done that denied fundamental democracy, no considerable number of Bolsheviks had any selfish impulse. It was this grand and goldenly hazy dream that fired them—the workers of all the world about to sweep into power and plenty, peace and joy, and for that cause the Bolsheviks would be perfectly willing to die.[5]

I think I may farther remark that this peculiar flowering could never be without a soil exactly suited for it, that Bolsheviks could never have been a great power in Russia if the Russian nature had not been peculiarly adapted to a dreamy altruism, gorgeous as the gold of sunset and as difficult to lay hold of. This is a world full of contradictions and anomalies, but the philosopher will not find any of them better food for meditation than the fact that the nation that has produced the most appalling cruelties has also produced men of the most extraordinary kindness, unselfishness, and broad, altruistic inspiration.

No doubt something is to be allowed in all this for the principle of compensations. The moment the horrible weight of the old system was lifted from the Russian, his heart and mind sprang up mountain high. This was but normal and wholesome. The

---

[5] This was indeed widely believed—and widely feared—at the time.

old regime had been to him the symbol of irresistible might, enduring pomp, chilling fear, savage and senseless cruelty. From the time he entered upon consciousness to the time he left the world, he drew no breath untainted with the poisonous effluvia of the thing, he saw no prospect free from its cold shadow. Of a sudden the right that he had thought eternal was removed; what he had taken for a symbol of everlasting power dissolved before his eyes. It seemed to him like the end of the old world and the beginning of the new. Whatever native unselfishness he had in his heart bloomed out into the belief that a change so tremendous ought to embrace all mankind, and the vision of an entirely new order for all the sons of men caught him full-heartedly. Nothing could have better fitted into his mood. Nevertheless, the Bolshevik movement, as an organized force, was always limited to the cities, chiefly Petrograd and Moscow. Bolshevik rank and file were factory and transport workers, and the great, significant and in the end determining fact remained that the peasant was not converted to the dream. For a time he might acquiesce in it—yes; but he would not accept the philosophy of it. He was a Revolutionist, he was a Socialist, he believed in eventual industrial democracy; but for the most part the dream of an instantaneous proletarian world left him untouched. Not even from the dazzling lure of the promised division of lands would he take fire, and it was evident that if Russia survived at all it would survive in other hands than the Bolsheviks' and without the golden vision.

But here once more, as so often before, the situation was exactly what the German propaganda could have wished. It gave to all the grandiose concepts of the Bolsheviks every possible assistance and much brilliant coloring. It led the unfortunate Trotskys by the hand through the economic Dreamland to the edge of the cliff and pushed them into the abyss. For it knew the Russian mind as a man knows the inside of his own house.[6]

It was much to know, for I may say it is a thing that has been the despair of most other foreigners. The contradiction I spoke of between a people of the kindliest impulses and their government given over to the most appalling cruelties is but one of a long list of utterly inconsistent qualities. Take a race that is at the same time prone to cheerfulness and prone to profound melancholy; full of optimistic hope and ready to despair; full in about equal proportions of confidence and fatalism; merry and gloomy; capable of tolerating the unspeakable barbarities of the imperial system and full at the same time of a feminine tenderness and sympathy with the least suffering; gentle and rough; hard fighters when they fight at all, but hating a fight and always hoping to avoid it; generous and parsimonious; elemental, and yet, about some things, the most sophisticated people on earth; and you can begin to respect the achievement of the Germans when they found out the key to such a psychology and were able to turn it to their own uses.

---

[6] Again, he attributes events to Germans, which was very popular in the case of the Bolsheviks.

By the common consent of all superficial visitors, the Russian is essentially lazy; being Oriental, he must be lazy; tradition would fail and our accepted and beloved theories yield no more of comfort to our souls if we could not call him lazy. And yet he can give on occasion the most astounding examples of industry, patient and plodding, also swift and long-continued. Similarly eminent are the authorities that have convinced us of the peasants' dullness. And yet they are continually showing great alertness of mind and great capacity for intelligent action. There is little dissent from the common verdict that the Russians as a whole are deficient in initiative. Yet the idea has been proved over and over to be grossly absurd, for the Russian soldier has shown on the field of battle an aptitude for initiative that confounds his critics.

In the historic retreat of the Russian forces from the Carpathians in the summer of 1915, for instance. Many Russian officers had been killed, many others had been found to be incompetent. Long sections of a line, stretched out over many leagues upon leagues, were without any general command. The army was executing one of the most difficult and perilous of maneuvers; it was fighting rear-guard actions as it retired before a superior foe that pressed it fiercely. Yet the Russians held the line intact and got home with losses so light that the world wondered. So marvelous, in fact, was the feat, the busy brains of the uneasy wights that are always looking for a Moses had to invent a hero for the occasion. They picked out the Grand Duke Nicholas as a fine figure for an idol and proceeded to spread the notion that he was the master-mind of the strategy.

The world accepted this engaging fiction and probably will ever cling to it. Yet in point of fact the celebrated Grand Duke had as much to do with the retreat as one of the horses that drew a gun. He went along, but he directed nothing. Correspondents that saw the whole performance told me that the Grand Duke's specialty was striking soldiers in the face and swearing at them. At these accomplishments he was as good as the best; otherwise he was of but barren achievement. The real heroes of the retreat were General Alexeev, who was undoubtedly a great military genius, and the Russian private, who understood what was required for safety and success and went ahead and provided it. I am even told that Russian soldiers without officers would pick the best places for the trench line, and dig themselves in, as well as they could have done under any skilled leadership.[7]

There is, of course, much in the Russian that seems to slower-pulsed people like extravagance and impulsiveness. Albert Thomas, at that time French Minister of Munitions, one of the great minds of his country and one of the ablest of living orators, visited Russia in the early summer of 1917, and created a profound impression. At the close of his speech it was usual for the people to arise and shout their approval, sometimes lifting him in their arms and carrying him in triumph through the streets.

---

[7] Pretty good description of the Grand Duke as commander and of the ability of General A. V. Alexseev, who became the formal commander of the armies in 1917 and then briefly fought the Bolsheviks in the early stages of the Civil War before being killed in battle.

He discovered after a time that the same people that paid him these honors would a short time later do much the same things for another orator expressing exactly opposite sentiments. This did not mean fickleness nor feebleness of mind, although it was so construed. It only meant that the people were applauding good oratory, of which classical art, by the way, they are excellent and discriminating judges, being themselves a nation of orators.[8]

This is another amazement, and a contradiction that may well cause us to ponder, since of course before the Revolution there was no free speech in Russia, and consequently how could such an art be practiced! In the processes of nature you would as soon expect pineapples to grow by the Lena River as a race of orators in silenced and fear-bound Russia. Yet observe the product. Such men as Chkheidze and Tsereteli in the full swing of oratorical triumph, the words rolling and thundering forth like a lava stream, burning and flashing, never a slip, never an instant's hesitation, the orator rising to new heights of passion and taking with him every hearer's rapt attention, vindicate the best traditions of a very noble art. Yet I do not know that these men were much more remarkable than a thousand others. Everybody is expected to talk well, and nothing is more illuminating about Russian psychology than the fact that to the Russian mind the oratory of most other countries is but cold and clammy. They look for rapidity, action, vehemence, overwhelming passion, winding up with "Hurrah!" for something, or "Long live!" something else.

When we were on our way back from Petrograd some misbegotten knaves, agents of Germany with whom Russia was so oversupplied, were alert enough to burn a bridge in front of our train in the hope that we should fall into the river and be killed. This failed, but we were held up thirty-six hours in a Russian town while the bridge was undergoing repair. In that time other low-lived minions of despotism tried four times to set our train on fire. They did not succeed in this, either, I am pleased to remark, but finally, to their own great satisfaction, no doubt, they were able to fire a warehouse by the side of our train with the manifest and wicked thought that we should be burned up with it. They had a device, the invention of the devil, their father, that consisted of a small sharp dagger and some concoction of phosphorus that would take fire from the sun's rays. They would stick this upon the side of a building and walk quietly off and when the building was afire they would be miles away.

They used this on the warehouse by the side of our train and the first thing we knew the structure was flaming.[9]

It was an excellent chance to see the Russian characteristics in unpremeditated display. The whole population ran to the place, yelling at top pitch, a practice that

---

[8] One of the features of 1917 was that there were continuous orators speaking in the streets as well as in more formal places!

[9] The kind of fires he describes here were typically blamed on Germans, the enemy, no matter what caused them.

ceased not while the fire burned, the belief being apparently that flames could be assuaged by vocalization. Yet they were not much excited; Russians are seldom hysterical; and they worked with almost superhuman energy to save property. At some risk to themselves they ran our train into a place of safety. Freight-cars standing closer to the warehouse immediately took fire. The report went around, and might easily have been true, that these cars and others were loaded with ammunition, in which case that would have been shortly a hot and unhealthy neighborhood. But the Russians were undismayed. They went into the thick of the flames, exposed themselves recklessly to danger, of which they seemed to be insensible, came near to being burned, and drew all the remaining cars away from those that were on fire—never ceasing to yell, while they worked like fiends. Their labors saved many valuable commodities, but fifteen cars were destroyed.

This scene was typically Russian. So was the fact that the town's fire apparatus, which was early on the scene, might have been effective in extinguishing a fire in a chicken coop but not in anything larger. So was the other fact, most instructive, that nobody stopped to give much heed to the fire apparatus, but all started with an instantaneous response to be useful and meet the emergency.

There was something else that an outsider might have noted with still more of philosophical wonder. According to the strange but widespread error previously noted, the Russians are deficient in the capacity for united effort. This is the result of shallow reasoning, but when all the facts are considered, not to be wondered at. Persons of this faith start with the truism that there are nineteen different nationalities and languages in Russia[10] and that consequently there can be no such thing as cohesion in national affairs; and as the people have never had any responsibility or experience in government there can never be any cohesion in local affairs either.

Count Witte[11] was largely responsible for this part of the fixed faith of America about Russian affairs. When he was here at the time of the Portsmouth Treaty, he was somewhat embarrassed by the questions put to him by reporters and other Americans concerning Russian autocracy and the ill-fated Revolution of 1905, which had but lately (and most unluckily) failed. He defended Russia's archaic government by declaring that nothing but an iron despotism and a rifle at every corner would keep such discordant elements from cutting one another's throats, and therefore autocracy was necessary for Russia and much to be admired.

Americans accepted this doctrine, as they usually, in their good nature, will accept any skillfully compounded sophism from any foreign visitor, and we all arrived

---

[10] Many, many more, in fact.

[11] Sergei Witte had risen as a leading expert on industrialization, and during the Revolution of 1905 he became head of the government. He was a moderate conservative, not the ultra conservative as Russell suggests. Many consider him the last really capable leader of tsarist Russia.

at the comfortable conclusion that the Russians never could work together and the Iron Fist was a pretty good institution—for them. Of course we did not wish it for ourselves. Count Witte probably knew better. Instead of the Russians having no capacity for united effort they have, as I pointed out in the chapter about cooperation, an unusual capacity of that kind. At this fire I am telling you of there must have been a thousand of them, yelling and working with ferocious energy, and instinctively working together. There was something strange about it. I naturally expected to see a group at one end of a car trying to pull it in one direction and another group at the other end trying to pull it in the other direction, with the like exhibitions of light-headed aberration. But in spite of the yelling there was little confusion, but only a kind of instinctive falling into line one with another and uniting to do the obvious and necessary thing. An American that had lived many years in Russia observed that this was usually manifested in village life whenever any crisis great or small came upon the community.

I am sure that Count Witte must have known better also when it comes to national affairs, because no one that has seen the old Duma, the Congress of Soviets or any other deliberative body of representative Russians, will take seriously the notion that the diverse races of Russia need any Iron Fist to keep them in order. The Council consisted of representatives of all these races and never had a jar on any racial lines. The typical Russian does not care much for racial differences. How could he when he has as little patriotism as any man alive? Count Witte must have chuckled to himself when he saw how some of the wisest men of the American press took seriously his little fable.

Yet at once we are projected against the other side of this matter, the invariable Russian contradiction. The typical Russian is not much impressed with racial differences, and yet there was Kishinev.[12] He allowed his Government in the imperial days to stain itself black for all time with the most monstrous racial persecutions that have ever been known outside of Turkey. Of course it is but justice to acknowledge that he had at that time very little to do with his Government and no adequate means of protest against anything it did. The world will be slow to think he could not have shown in some way that he did not approve of wholesale murder. Yet here also the world will be wrong again. As soon as Russia was free, as soon as the hateful and insane old tyranny was beaten forth and democracy took its place, the Jew was endowed with all his natural rights as a citizen exactly like any other citizen. All restrictions were removed as to residence, utterance, or travel, and at least twenty-five Jews sat as elected delegates in the National Council. The Russian had made amends in his own peculiar way, which is an Oriental way and quite different from our way, but not therefore necessarily worse. Moreover, we shall have to accept him with his way, peculiar and

---

[12] Kishinev was the site of a major anti-Jewish pogrom in 1903. It now is the capital of Moldova.

intricate as that is, because unless Germany succeeds in suppressing him he has come among us to stay and be accounted with, we may be sure of that.

He has so many fine and good traits, this new democrat of the North, that it is impossible not to love him in spite of what to cooler temperaments seem startling inconsistencies. Show a typical Russian a chance to save life or avert disaster and he will leap into danger with the most magnificent disregard of his own safety. The people of Sicily are not likely soon to forget that fact. In the great earthquake of 1908 a Russian cruiser happened to be in harbor. The sailors swarmed ashore, went into toppling buildings, crawled over insecure walls, dug like mad in the ruins, worked day and night without sleep, and rescued hundreds of persons that must otherwise have perished. They not only appeared to the wonder-stricken Sicilians like great blond giants providentially sent to do wonders of physical strength and courage, but they worked intelligently and with invention, discovering new and startling ways of reaching places supposed to be inaccessible.

It was perfectly characteristic of them that they treated the unfortunate inhabitants with affectionate tenderness like that of mothers, ministering to the wounded, carrying little children or old folk to places of safety; and just as characteristic that, without the least remorse or compunction, they shot down anybody that came within the prohibited area. So it was in the Revolution. The people that fought the police with such desperate and ferocious courage, beating them to death so long as they offered resistance, throwing them into the canal, shooting them down without mercy, were the same people that would not injure the remnant police that surrendered, hated though these were.

Because he inherits a strong sense of justice and generosity, the Russian may be called a good sport. He fights powerfully, as a rule he fights intelligently, but he would scorn to maltreat a prisoner in his hands. Not even the terrible and authentic narratives of the sufferings of Russian prisoners in German camps provoked the least retaliation upon the 1,500,000 German and Austrian prisoners that were held in Russia. As a rule the German prisoner in Russia fared exceedingly well. I ought to know; I saw thousands upon thousands of them and talked with not a few. In some regions of Siberia they might be said to swarm over the landscape. I never saw one of them that did not seem to be well-nourished. His uniform might have grown ragged and his cap be faded or greasy, but he was physically fit and frequently well content.

Private soldiers that were prisoners in Russia were allowed to go forth to work. Many were employed upon the railroads, great numbers upon the farms, some in the factories and some seemed to roam the roads at their own sweet will. It was different with officers; they were confined within the stockades. I do not know how courtesy to a prisoner could further go than to make him a citizen, endow him with a ballot and elect him to sit as a legislator in the local council. German and Austrian prisoners in many parts of Russia immediately after the Revolution went through that experience, which was both Quixotic and eminently Russian, and many of them were still holding seats in the local governing bodies when I was there.[13]

I think it was an ominous but generally disregarded symptom that the Russians in 1917 showed plainly they had no feeling against the Germans and, what was still more important, they cared little or nothing about the racial ties supposed to bind them to the Serbians. This was a fact that many visitors could not understand, but fact it was nevertheless. The explanation was that the Revolution had raised the wild hope of an end to all nationalism and they thought to begin the new order at home. I will not be sure that to remember this particular tie would have been inconvenient, but as neither man nor nation does anything for only one reason such a view might have had weight. But as to the Germans, not Belgium, nor the violated faith, nor the slaves of Lille could win in my time any response from an average Russian audience. There was (a fact too commonly overlooked) a strong sentimental attraction toward Germany growing out of the German origin of the sacred doctrines of Socialism, and then there was the universal conviction that the German people were about to revolt, throw off the autocracy and proclaim the German Republic. I was never done wondering at the extent to which this delusion went. One day at luncheon with three of the most intelligent members of the Lvov cabinet, well-informed men, Messrs. Tsereteli, Chernov and Skobelev, I found these so thoroughly and honestly convinced the German Revolution was at hand that most of the conversation dwelt fondly upon the details of it. "Any moment we may get the news," said M. Skobelev. "It may be coming over the wires this instant."[14]

It seemed to me that there was much more feeling against the British than against the Germans, partly due to the efforts of the German agents, partly to resentment against what were believed to be the British tactics in Russia and partly to the general belief that Great Britain's one aim in entering the war was to secure the German colonies. There was no good will toward the Japanese but less hostility than I had looked for. Yet there was a general uneasiness about the future relations between the two countries. But the Russian as a rule does not cling with persistence or bitterness to any nationalistic prejudices. He has too much of the stoic philosophy in his strangely complex nature; also too much of the fatalist. Thus, fighting hard, he will hold to a hopeless corner longer than almost any other tribe on earth would stick there, and then give up fighting in an instant, sit down and take with the speechless fortitude of a North American Indian whatever fate may have in store—death, torture, or starvation in a prison camp. I was told that Russian prisoners in German hands never

---

[13] German and Austrian prisoners were indeed put to work in Russia before 1917, and some who were socialists got actively involved politically in 1917, but he exaggerates the amount.

[14] Belief that the Russian Revolution would inspire revolution elsewhere, especially in Germany, was widespread in Russia in 1917 and 1918. Ironically, the Russian revolutions, especially the Bolshevik one, helped stimulate an unsuccessful one in Germany in 1918 at the end of World War I.

gave their guards any trouble, never complained, never asked for anything different, but merely folded their arms and dropped out when they could stand no more. Until that time, among the sick in the prison, the wounded, the suffering, the kindest of all nurses and warmest of friends were these same Russians.

Yet turn the next way and you will find him looking with cold and indifferent eyes upon another scene of suffering. The brutality in the Russian army and navy, which I have described in a former chapter, never called forth any protest from anybody of purely Russian origin, although it had that effect upon some others. I know of a young officer in the Russian navy whose mother was an American and whose American blood once revolted against the savagery around him, and revolted in a way that cost him dear. He was making his first cruise as an ensign. At a Baltic port the vessel stopped to take on a certain number of raw recruits. Two officers were stationed at the head of the ladder. As each new man landed upon the deck one officer dealt him a stunning blow with the clenched fist aimed at his ear and the other kicked him off his feet.

The semi-American ensign viewed this with horror and wrath and tore up to the bridge to protest against it to the commanding officer. He only succeeded in having himself ordered to the lazarette for ten days.

"Monstrous impudence!" said the commanding officer, aghast. "What do you mean by coming up here to teach me my duty?"

Fatalism is strong upon the Russian; he has a powerful instinct to view whatever is as having been ordained for him and not to be combated until the same Fates relent or open up a way to get rid of the affliction. This is utterly inconsistent with the marvelous story of the Russian Revolutionary fight, which for relentless tenacity through many years has no equal in human history. Inconsistent—yes; but nearly everything in Russia is inconsistent with something else. Inconsistency is one of the Russian's strongest traits and helps to make him lovable and human. After a time you get so you do not mind his inconsistencies, but develop a certain pleasurable sense in the taste of them, their piquant frankness and their variety, ever fresh and new. When he makes an appointment with someone for 3 o'clock at his office and at 2:30 wanders out and does not return, his eccentricities may seem somewhat annoying to the visitor but the Russian cannot for the life of him see why they should be. There is tomorrow, or next week or next month. Come around again. If he happens to think of it next time he may be on hand.

Yet he is very far from being a thoughtless or irrational creature and still farther from any lack of consideration for his fellow-man. He is naturally reflective, likes to weigh argument against argument, and will admit with candor a change in his views. On the train with us from Vladivostok to Petrograd was a certain American whose coming was known in advance to the Revolutionists of a large Siberian city. They wanted to get his views about a matter of moment to them, and sent to meet him at the station the head of the civil council governing the city and the head of the soldiers' organization. This illuminating conversation followed:

"Do you think we did right," asked the Russians, "in supporting the provisional government at Petrograd?

"Most assuredly," said the American. "Why not?"

"But it contains capitalists."

"Well, so does the world, but we are to live in it just the same. So does Russia, but you don't leave it on that account."

"That is very true, but do you think we can properly sit down at the same council-table with capitalists?"

"Why not? In the present emergency you and the capitalist members of the Government have exactly the same object, and that object must be attained before anything else."

"What do you think it is?"

"Why, plainly enough, to make democracy secure here. The great danger that you face is from without. Democracy is in no particular danger from within. Nobody in Russia will restore the Tsar. But if Germany gets the upper hand in Russia, she absolutely must bring back the old regime or something like it, for the simple, obvious reason that she cannot afford to have a democracy stretched along her northern frontier. It would mean the overthrow of her own system of absolutism. For her sheer safety she must have absolutism here. Imagine Germany between the Republic of France on the south and the Republic of Russia on the north. How long would the Kaiser last? The very first essential for democracy in Russia is that you shall keep Germany out."

A silence ensued in which it was evident the Russians were turning this to and fro in their minds. Then they announced that it was good, making the announcement in the Russian fashion, which consisted of kissing the American suddenly upon both cheeks and inviting him to come back as soon as possible, have more tea and talk more in the same line.

When the Russian makes an engagement, forgets to keep it, and his attention is called to the lapse, his theory is that the Fates have merely ordained that he shall walk out of his office at a certain time and out he walks accordingly. There was an apt illustration of his fatalism in the Bolshevik rebellion of October, 1917. As I have previously explained, the whole Government of Russia at that time rested in the hands of the All-Russian Congress of Soviets and was never vested in Kerensky or in the ministry. When the Congress adjourned it left as the governing power in Russia an executive committee of 250 persons, membership being apportioned among the political parties in exact ratio to their strength in the Soviet. This gave, I think, the Bolsheviks and Maximalists 38 or 39 members in the Executive Committee, all the rest of which was anti-Bolshevik.[15] When the Bolsheviks made their armed uprising, seized the machinery of government in Petrograd, declared Kerensky deposed and Lenin prime minister in his place, the anti-Bolsheviks in the Executive Committee said:

"Oh, very well! If you want to do this kind of thing, go ahead."

So they withdrew in a body from the committee, leaving the minority rump of Bolsheviks to command the situation unopposed and to represent themselves to be both the Executive Committee and the National Soviet, being, in truth, neither.

Meantime their opponents, although they were a majority,[16] sat down quietly to wait until Fate and a general election should bring in their revenge. And while they waited, Petrograd, in spite of what you may have heard, remained for the most part orderly, for that would be the Russian of it. The Government might be shifting from Menshevik to Bolshevik and back from Bolshevik to Menshevik, but through it all life and property would be safer than in almost any other city undergoing the like experiences.[17]

But of all the incidents that pertain to the Russian psychology the favorite for dramatic interest and punch ought to be the story of the *Nicholas Potemkin*.[18] This was a powerful armored cruiser of the Black Sea fleet. Her sailors had been treated for some years to the peculiar and savage cruelty that prevailed in the Russian naval service of that time and had borne it all with the national fortitude and stoicism. Not a Russian officer seemed ever to have suspected that men might resent such treatment. The universal belief among the officers was that to beat and kick the foremast men was a salutary and useful exercise and to be enjoyed to the limit, and the men themselves, since they said nothing about it, must admit that it was good for them to be kicked and beaten.

---

[15] This section is somewhat confused. By fall 1917, a Bolshevik-led coalition gained a majority in and took over the Petrograd Soviet, the de facto most important institution. Mensheviks and SRs still held the majority of the Executive Committee of the All-Russian Congress of Soviets, which had met in May, and about which he talks mostly in referencing the Soviet leadership. Elections had been held for the Second Congress, resulting in the Bolsheviks being the largest party and leaders of a radical left majority. On the eve of its meeting, an armed action by Kerensky against the Soviet stimulated a popular uprising that left the Bolsheviks in control of the congress and the new government created out of it.

[16] As noted, the Bolsheviks' opponents were NOT the majority at the Second Congress. They did, however, expect to control the Constituent Assembly in January 1918.

[17] It did not shift back to Menshevik. Elections to the Constituent Assembly, which met in January 1918, had a SR majority, but it was disbanded by the Bolsheviks. What Russell is saying reflects what a lot of people widely believed would happen at the time he wrote.

[18] He now radically changes subjects, going back to the 1905 revolution. The revolt of the *Potemkin* crew was indeed a major event of the Revolution of 1905 and topic of later Russian history. His account is rather romanticized, and in fact, the crew did end up taking the ship into a foreign port and many of them lived long lives, sometimes as part of revolutionary parties.

Of a sudden, on June 23, 1905, the world was electrified with the news that the crew of the *Potemkin* had mutinied, seized the vessel, killed most of her officers, locked up the rest, and was then cruising around the Black Sea under commanders elected by the forecastle. For the next four days all reading mankind followed with breathless interest the career of the mutineers. They appeared at night off Odessa and bombarded it, apparently for luck. They encountered several vessels of the imperial navy and fought so fiercely that the Tsar's ships were sunk or driven into flight. They went up and down the coast, spreading terror but doing no great harm. They sent ashore to the municipality of Odessa and to other places messages of contempt mixed with a grim kind of humor. Under the direction of a bright young officer whose life they had spared they maneuvered their ship with exceeding skill. He subsequently wrote an account of the voyage that for vivid interest and incredible adventures came near to beating anything extant. The men did not get drunk and did not commit excesses; they merely sailed to and fro, took potshots at the Tsar's ships and had a right good time playing at freedom.

Of course it could not last, for the Tsar's Government was gathering in hot haste an overwhelming naval force to master the rebels. The obvious thing to do was to put into a foreign port, get ashore and make on foot for a place of safety. Having rebelled against the authority of their country they would have been entitled to the position of political refugees. The young officer saw what was coming and urged the mutineers to look out for themselves, run into a foreign port (there were several handy) and miss the gallows while there was a chance. They refused absolutely to listen to him, not because they were drunk but because they wanted to have more fun with the Tsar's ships before they quit.

Then the officer, having uncomfortable visions of himself swinging at the end of a rope, dropped overboard into a boat and made his escape. If the rest had been equally wise many of them might be living today. They stuck to the ship and continued the cruise, breathing defiance and looking for imperial vessels to sink. Finally they saw themselves surrounded by irresistible forces. Fate had called for them. They ran the *Potemkin* straight into a Russian port, walked ashore, put their heads into the waiting nooses and were hanged.

Climate has much to do with the Russian's peculiarities; "we are what suns and winds and waters make us." In a country of long, gray, gloomy winters what should we expect but melancholy? And in a country of extreme cold alternating with almost tropical heat we should naturally expect some reflection in the temperament and sensibilities of the people. Incessant battling against bitter winter weather must be responsible for both the tenacity and endurance of these people, and may equally be the origin of their fatalism. But as even the cold of Irkutsk chills no whit the hospitality of the native there, neither will any of the Russian's little ways that are all his own lessen the liking that all men have for him that know him well, nor interfere with the work in the world he seems destined to do.

THE BOLSHEVIK

He has an extraordinary musical sense and a delicate ear for harmony. Long ago he discovered, I know not how, a fact hardly yet recognized in the Western world, that every building has its own musical pitch, and the discovery is one of the secrets of his marvelous church music that has been praised so oft and oft and still, to my thinking, not enough. For instance, part of the church service consists of alternating recitative and chant. In such a building as the great Kazan Cathedral, where on June 18, 1917, was celebrated a special service in honor of the American Commission, there is a very long, reverberating echo that adjusts itself to the building's pitch, and finishes upon it. When it dies out the recitative starts upon exactly that note, so that it seems to be a revival of the echo still lingering in the listener's mind.

Yet while he is susceptible to sweet music and especially to sad, and often is visibly moved at it in his church, I found him not often an extreme religionist and seldom anything of a bigot. He seems to find no great fault with another man's style of faith. There are in Petrograd churches of about all the leading kinds in the world, including a large and handsome Mohammedan mosque. Since, in the way before described, the Revolution has so marvelously remade and democratized the Russian's own church, it no longer interferes in government and politics. This is a change very wonderful, because in the old days it was the strong bulwark of the existing system. For the time being, anyway, Revolutionary Government and the Church agreed to let each other alone. It seems strange, but by at least a great part of the hierarchy the new order was viewed with satisfaction, which merely presents another Russian contradiction. In the old regime the Church was a mighty power. After the Revolution it was not a civil power at all, and everybody was content to have it so.[19]

Exceptions can be found to nearly anything in Russia. I have been speaking here of types. While Russians of different types and orders of mind differed about thousands of things, Bolsheviks, Mensheviks, Trudoviks, the land question, syndicalism, ownership in common, and so to the end of a long catalogue, I found three things that practically all of them (aside from the old privileged classes) had in common and in about equal degrees. These were essential kindness of heart, a fund of common-sense and a fervent profession of democracy.

Russians are among the most likable people on earth. Putting aside some peculiarities, such as their fatalism and some of their stoicism, there is another race that they strongly resemble. That stout old warrior General Clay was right; it is the American. Probably we can understand the Russian better than anybody else can understand him and we ought to do it.[20]

---

[19] Churches did indeed gain a new independence after the overthrow of the monarchy. The Russian Orthodox Church was undergoing a major restructuring during the time he was there. The new conditions did not last long after the Bolsheviks took power.

[20] These ideas of Russian-American similarities were common at the time.

Chapter IX
The Influence of Manners and Morals

If the shade of Thomas Babington Macaulay was haunting these confines in the summer of 1906, it must have returned hence to cause in spirit-land the echoes of an inextinguishable laughter.[1]

While still he wore these fleshly cerements [burial garments] it was the opinion of this eminent authority that the most comical thing on earth was the spectacle of the British public in one of its periodical spasms of aggressive virtue. In the summer of 1906 he could have seen in the United States a specimen of aggressive virtue that would have made any exhibition he ever witnessed from the British branch of the Grundy Family[2] look like a shameful surrender to vice.

Also he could have seen the American public playing into the hands of an arch-enemy of this nation, and while that particular part of the show might have been funny to him, there subsequently seemed to be very little fun in it for the thoughtful American.

It was the occasion of the far-famed and historic visit of Maxim Gorky to these United States.[3] Mr. Gorky had many friends and ardent admirers here and seems to have come over in a spirit of innocent eagerness, expecting a cordial welcome in the land of the free. These happy expectations were dashed to earth, and long after they had passed and been forgotten one of the Tsar's army of spies and secret agents that then covered the earth with a network of villainy told the instructive story of exactly how Mr. Gorky's disappointment was achieved.

The Tsar's government hated Gorky and had long yearned to destroy him, but never quite dared. He was one of the bold and relentless Revolutionary leaders of Rus-

---

[1] Russell is preparing to write an elaborate comment on events. Macaulay was a British historian and politician who wrote on many subjects.

[2] A narrow-minded person who excessively criticizes the conduct of others.

[3] Gorky is perhaps still today the most famous of Russian fiction authors of the time. He had been forced to live abroad for many years of the late tsarist regime. During that time, he made a trip to the United States and became the serious target of conservative newspapers, which left him anti-US for the rest of his life. In 1917, he returned to Russia and became deeply involved in leftist politics, including editing an influential newspaper. He played a major role in developing early Soviet era fiction.

sia, heroic figures too audacious and too conspicuous to be made before the world's gaze victims of the blood-soaked machine by which autocracy retained its power in a country that loathed it. Once it had attempted to wreak its vengeance on him, arresting him on a trumped-up charge, but the outside world made such a protest that even Tsarism was affrighted and the novelist was released. Thereafter he took no chances on the autocratic conception of justice and lived in Italy. By common report he had been separated but not divorced from his legal wife; he brought to this country a lady with whom he was alleged or supposed to associate informally and minus the sanction of the marriage tie; and the spy thought he knew the American psychology well enough to be able to use this fact to the novelist's undoing.

In the disguise of a simple American of stern moral principles, he protested to a New York newspaper against allowing this person, that thus openly flaunted his shame in our faces, to land upon our unpolluted shores, and in twenty-four hours the hunt was up and away. Bravely it coursed up and down in pursuit of the lonely and unfortunate Russian, who found every hotel door shut in his face and was literally reduced to tramping the streets until private persons that were willing to dare the storm of criticism opened their houses to shelter him. Never, I suppose, has Virtue been so triumphantly vindicated in this our broad land. One can almost imagine her majestic figure returning victorious from the conflict, her lofty glance still threatening all evildoers as she waved her mighty and irresistible sword in air.

But much more was involved in this incident than the triumph of statutory and traditional morality. I do not know that the spy ever sensed the fact, but he could never have achieved such a feat in America on purely moral grounds, moral as we believe ourselves nevertheless. The truth is, Mr. Gorky was well known in certain circles of this country to be a social reformer of advanced ideas concerning economics. It was then the fashion to try to discredit all such reformers. One method was to make it appear that they were all believers in the pernicious doctrine of free love, and if the story of Maxim Gorky's private life had been manufactured to order it could not have better pleased men and journals of this disposition. So they accepted with joy this apparent gift of the gods, and did a complete and satisfactory job, and discredited Gorky, and made his stay in this country perfectly hellish, and sent him home sourly resentful, and were contented and happy ever after.

But in a way they never suspected they had hit the interests and perhaps the welfare of their own country a heavy blow. Mr. Gorky went home with a heart full of bitterness; also of contempt and what he deemed to be disillusion about America. From one point of view he had some reason for his contempt. If he ever cared to read the records of the divorce courts in the city that spurned him as unfit for human society, or if he listened to the comments of the sophisticated, he could not have failed to see that the pretense of morality in the persecution he had suffered was exceedingly shallow. Anyway, he went back, the determined enemy of the United States. He wielded one of the most powerful pens in the world. He had also great and commanding influence in his native country. His story of the treatment he had received and his account of conditions in America made a profound impression upon the Russian mind. It was not changed by after events and by the close of 1917 Americans were in a good position to judge of its results.

True, the social reformer had been well discredited, but there seemed fair reasons to wish that his private affairs had been let alone.

From his account of his experiences all thinking Russia went to two conclusions. First, that America was a country of "bourgeois morals" and second, that its press and its governing machinery were absolutely controlled by the capitalists.

If it was a country of bourgeois morals, then it was hopelessly unenlightened; and if it was controlled by the capitalists, then it was hopelessly backward.[4]

When the Revolution broke, Mr. Gorky was chief owner of a newspaper in Petrograd, the *Novaia Zhizn*. It speedily attained a great circulation and great influence. In it he expressed for the United States the bitter dislike and scornful contempt he not unnaturally felt for it, and his journal helped greatly to bring about that condition of misunderstanding between the two countries that produced such lamentable results. Without ever intending it or knowing it, he was a powerful assistant to the propaganda and cohorts from the East Side of New York that in the German interest went to Russia to make trouble.

I am not to be understood as championing Mr. Gorky's supposed convictions as to the necessity for the marriage ceremony, or as making any judgment upon them. His views on that subject are his own private affair and none of my business. I try here only to make Americans understand Russia, and it is impossible to do that without touching on the topic thus suggested, unconventional as it is for ordinary and frank discussion before a mixed audience.

Any man that has traveled open-eyed about this world knows well enough that what we call morality is largely geographical. Civilization as we have thus far known it has certain fixed bases of faith between nation and nation and man and man, such as those that Germany in 1914 and thereafter sought to overturn and trample upon in war; but when it comes to the morality of the relations between the sexes, that is a different matter. What is perfectly moral at one degree of longitude becomes grossly and intolerably immoral at another. What one nation regards with indifference another looks upon with shudders, and I do not believe we shall ever get far in international accord until we come to some recognition of this fact. We are not obliged to adopt or admire the ideas of another country but we may as well admit that, like our own, they are the product of environment and training and cannot be eradicated to order.

That being the case, there is no occasion for the petrified horror with which some American and most British visitors view what they call the moral condition of a city

---

[4] The Gorky affair was indeed unfortunate, and made some Russians unhappy with the United States, but the event did not have as negative an impact on relations as this suggests. Russell would have picked this up in Russia in 1917.

like Petrograd. According to the Russian standards it is not the "most immoral city in the world." It is not immoral at all. With a perfectly naive sincerity the Russians look upon these things in a way different from our way. They see nothing wrong in certain things that seem very wrong to us, and as their standards will have to continue to be their own and not ours we gain nothing by berating them.

Yet the Nevsky Prospekt after sundown is not a place where men that understand the terrible significance of prostitution will be really glad to be.[5] Neither is Piccadilly, for that matter, nor a hundred other streets in the heart of London. But here it is with a difference; a meretricious commerce is carried on with complete frankness and to the utter unconcern of those not directly engaged in it. The sale of popcorn or peanuts might attract more attention.

It is a point of view of which the morals of the Nevsky Prospekt are only one reflection. Taking Russia by and large, one may say that as a rule, where there is no implication of force or fraud and no interference with social rank, what we call illicit relations between the sexes are regarded as not morally objectionable. That is the fact, baldly stated. But if you ask me for an opinion as to the practical results of such a view of a very tangled and difficult problem I shall have to say frankly that I do not think it works well. Every country has its own customs, says the wise French proverb. I have no idea of setting an example in the criticism about which I have just been finding fault. The Russians are entitled to their own view of the matter and to be happy in it if they can. But without going into needless details there are certain facts about the way this laxity works out well known to everybody that knows Russia and not exhilarating to those that wish the country well. A man need not be squeamish or unduly sensitive about such things to wish much success to White Cross and other movements for sexual restraint after contemplating some of these conditions. Laying aside any question of morals, in any state of society that is designed to be stable and wholesome, it would seem, for instance, well to discourage a habit among young girls of visiting the rooms of male guests at hotels, and also to check, so far as possible, the spread of social diseases. I suggest but two aspects of the matter. There are others.

One great difficulty about mentioning this phase of Russian life is that immediately the reactionary will parrot his favorite remarks that the Russian's idea of liberty is license, and that the Russian people, being entirely unfitted for freedom, cut loose in a libidinous carnival as soon as the restraining hand of the imperial government was removed. These assertions, although continually made in this country, were baseless. There was no "license" and no carnival of libidinous extravagance. Every condition that seems shocking now to the delicate soul of a prunes-and-prisms Anglo-Saxon existed no less under the empire. The Revolution brought no enlarged freedom in these respects and had no effect upon what we should call the morals of the country

---

[5] The main street of Petrograd/St. Petersburg and also the business center. It is worth noting that most of the pictures of major marches and demonstrations of 1917 are located there. There was legal prostitution in Russia at the time, and—given war conditions—illegal as well.

except what might result from an increased seriousness of mental habit. Instead of license being any result of the Revolution, the most amazing thing was the evidence among the people everywhere of an unequaled capacity for restraint and self-control. But probably nothing will ever remove the other idea from the average American mind. It is fixed there with the belief in universal Russian "illiteracy" and ignorance of and unfitness for democracy and the rest of the misconceptions that have wrought so much trouble between the two countries. It gratifies our prejudices and preconceived ideas to believe these fantasies; what then shall hinder us from believing them!

The Russian is an Oriental;[6] that may help those of us that wish to solve his riddle. No doubt he has an Oriental idea of what we call sexual morality. But at the very next turn we are laid all aback with the fact that he is not the least Oriental in his attitude toward the place of women in society; new Russia was one of the first nations to adopt woman suffrage, an inconsistency that ought to, but will not, give pause to the confident souls that so easily draw generalities about him. What! Shall we give up choice indoor sport merely because the Russian is a sphinx and fails to make good our excellent prognoses?

But as to what we call morals, of course the standards of the Nevsky Prospekt after sundown are reflected in the powerful Russian literature and the extraordinary Russian drama. There are those among us that are willing to take the Russian novel as it is and slip off our Puritan scruples for the sake of the Russian novelist's unequaled grasp upon the vital and the moving; for when you read him it is as if one of Bret Harte's "jinnies fierce and wild" had reached out of space and caught you irrevocably by the heart.[7] And as to the drama, if I may make any fair guess, that is no more than beginning, and another generation is likely to see Russian plays that will set the world agape, morals or no morals. But I speak of the people as they are today, and according to all tradition and theory one of the best reflexes of their mental state should be found in a typical audience at a theater or a typical group of spectators at a film show.

But I solemnly swear to you I went out upon such a hunt and returned but little wiser. There was at one of the larger film theaters of Petrograd when I was there a moving-picture show that certainly should bring out a people's mental processes, if anything of that kind could. It was a version of the Russian Revolution and the story of Rasputin.[8] Morals aside, once more, the thing was exceedingly well done; there is no question about that. The acting seemed to be superbly spirited; the stirring scenes of the Revolution were put on with endless accessories, great crowds and potent realism. Night after night the theater was packed with people. They sat there and

---

[6] "Oriental" was at the time a term for Asian, or just "Eastern" people and places.

[7] Bret Harte was a famous American short story writer of the nineteenth century, especially about the American West.

[8] The revolution opened up a world of uncensored film. There were many on the revolution and with negative pictures of Rasputin and the royal family.

gazed upon vivid picturings of the most colossal drama in modern history and of the strangest and weirdest tale ever told, and for emotion might as well have been graven of stone.

I could not then explain this fact and do not pretend to explain it now. I went back to the place more than once to make sure, and I talked with others that went, some of them as much puzzled as I, and it was always the same story. The people sat absolutely unmoved before scenes that one would think would stir them to their depths. There was every kind of strong, if primitive, emotion in that play, also everything calculated to appeal to the Revolutionary spirit of Revolutionists and the reactionary spirit of reactionaries, and nobody seemed to be either glad or mad.

They saw the alleged relations between Rasputin and the late Tsarina indicated with a frankness and lack of reserve that might have appalled a crowd of Westerners, but these apparently were neither shocked nor pleased. They saw the late Tsar depicted as dull, sensual, cruel and as his wife's degraded dupe, and if there were monarchists in the company they did not care, and if there were republicans they suppressed their elation. They saw the Tsar signing his abdication and surrendering the throne of his ancestors and were unconcerned. They saw the uprising of the people, the dawn of liberty, the fighting in the streets, the triumph of democracy, the longlooked-for day come at last, the long processions of cheering multitudes, and gave never a handclap.

I could never well understand that play. The author might with equal reason be believed to have planned it to awaken enthusiasm for the Revolution or sympathy for the deposed and worthless tribe of Romanovs—I never could tell which. The Tsar in the earlier scenes was represented as unattractive, but the last scenes seemed intended to make him a martyr and a figure of cheap pathos, if anybody cares for that. He is a prisoner in his palace; he paces up and down with bent head, and then tries to pass out of a doorway. Two soldiers, with bayonets advanced, halt him. He nods his head and sighs, and then paces around to another door and two other soldiers halt him there. Then he draws apart the window curtains and looks sadly into the street where the people are celebrating the Revolution, and the end of it is a "close up" of him in that position.

One night a young officer, pointed out to me as the son of a noble, shed tears at this rather mawkish scene, but the rest of the people did not cry nor seem to care. It was plain that they were interested, but whatever emotions they felt they successfully concealed.

On another occasion I saw a film of a celebrated American comic hero of the movies whose impossible and galumphing antics have made millions roar in this country, and he did not seem funny to the Russians. They observed him chasing cannon-balls and dancing on his head and did not even smile. This time it was plain they were bored by the show. They talked and moved restlessly about and cracked sunflower seeds, and some went out, a signal proof of disapprobation, for the Russian is thrifty; he will not easily spend money for a show and then leave it.

Yet a few nights later I saw an audience composed of about the same class of people made ecstatic by a vocalist. He sang very effectively some Russian folksongs and the people cheered him with a sincerity of feeling that any performer might be proud to evoke. They were discriminating, also; they knew good singing from a poorer offering; they were not carried away by any bare appeal of the song itself. Being singers themselves they had reason to know the real from the counterfeit. A little later they would hardly give a hand to a performer that they thought fell short of a laudable standard.

It was a very large audience and a program that began at 8:30 P.M. lasted until 1 A.M., which in summer is no unusual time for these entertainments to close. A man made the audience cry with the way he read a simple little poem. I doubt if anybody could make an American audience cry with the same thing. Another man made them laugh with a comic sketch of his own composing. I think this was the most interesting part of the performance. The sketch being new there was an unusual chance to see how the minds of the people worked upon a humorous suggestion and they seemed to work like a steel trap. They seized the idea the instant it left the speaker's lips.

They laughed at funny lines, wept at a poem about a little girl in the snow, and looked with considerable indifference on film-show antics of a high-priced and favorite entertainer.

Before the Revolution the censorship of plays was very strict, but only in relation to their political significance. Cut out any suggestion of revolution or disloyalty or lack of perfect servility toward the divinely chosen tribe of parasites, and one could go as far as one pleased. In many cases this was pretty far. George Bernard Shaw's *Mrs. Warren's Profession*, that play at which the foundations of English morality were supposed to rock, was given in Russia without the least difficulty. Only, people did not like it and its run was short. I was at pains to ask what was thought to be the matter with it and was told that the Russians could not see anything in it. It seemed to them but a flat, colorless and dreary thing, without adequate reason. They could think of no basis upon which anyone should find entertainment in such a play. I suppose what they were trying to say was that it lacked punch, and indeed, compared with some of the admired Russian dramas, it does look somewhat pale and without a clutch. Some of my Russian friends thought I must be in error when I said that *Mrs. Warren's Profession* had been suppressed by the British authorities. The task of making them understand why was beyond my powers and patience. I could not induce them to believe that anybody thought that play immoral. It is not that they have a lower sense of morality but that theirs is different. The great thing in Russian art of any kind is Power; nothing else counts much. Let an artist deal with the relations of the sexes or deal with a birch forest in dead winter, but whatever he deals with, he is to let go with all he has and be not afraid, nothing will bite him. That seems to be the controlling idea and some of the results take the breath of the modern world.

Painting, for instance. They opened, especially for us one morning the Alexander II Museum of Modern Russian Art, that overpowering place of wonders into which not even the most careless ever strolled without emerging in a swirl of new emotions and strange visions. It was all here; the beginning of modern Russian painting, timid and imitative; the slickery styles of a century ago conscientiously transplanted like hothouse growths to an uncongenial soil; then the awakening when the Russians found themselves and their own methods, and behold these miles of canvases to make all the world wonder. Power—power and subtlety and the most amazing perception of the inside things of life, life everywhere else as much as in Russia, things that you always felt were there but never before saw put into a picture, great scenes with the most daring but most successful color schemes, portraits that had underneath amazing sardonic suggestions of the vanity and sordidness of life; but everything done with power. No punch, no picture, is the Russian rule. It is not worth while merely to paint something that is pretty or nice. The nice little thing is ill esteemed in Russia. Come down with a smash—but right on the center of the target.[9]

And the same people that have such an unerring intuitive sense of truth about art and cannot be fooled out of it, can be led into economic and political dreamland by persons that tell them the Heavenly Utopia is due at noon tomorrow and with the waving of a magic wand, behold the golden streets and hark the symphony of harps!

Also, we descend with a thump from the magnificent altitudes of Russian art as displayed in modern paintings to the kind of Russian art that is represented in the comic illustrated newspapers, some of which navigate the streams of the gutter. As soon as the lid fell off the press with the collapse of the empire, out came a swarm of these publications, joyously released from the least restraint. I made a collection of them while I was in Russia and some were of a nature to cause the grave of Anthony Comstock to break into eruption.[10] No doubt it is all a matter of the point of view, as I have said before, but my argument of the point of view I must stretch pretty far (I confess it) to be able to cover some of the things the comic artists draw weekly for their inured constituents. The raft of it is pretty coarse stuff and not discernibly funny to the Western mind, but the Russians smile at it. Yet we should go slow about drawing any conclusions from that fact. I have seen worse things in Berlin and in the Munich

---

[9] It is interesting that he was so impressed by the art he saw. One would like to think he saw some of the abstract art that was emerging at that time—Kazimir Malevich, Vladimir Tatlin, Natalia Goncharova, and others—but probably it was the earlier (but still great) art of people like Valentin Serov and Ilya Repin.

[10] An American nineteenth century crusader against books, pictures, and other things he believed to be indecent. The 1873 Comstock Act was a sweeping act that included a federal ban on contraceptives.

Salon of 1913, and every visitor that has trod observingly the Alte Wiese at Carlsbad is immune against shock from the Russian comics.

I was rather astonished to see that the Rasputin story still furnished these jesters with endless material, of a broad, ancient and gargantuan style of humor. A favorite achievement was to represent, with some details that I omit, Rasputin carrying the Empress off in his arms while the Tsar stood by and looked on, loutishly helpless.[11] You may remember that they laughed at similar things on the immortal road from Southwark at the Tabard to Canterbury, about six hundred years ago. It was now become one of the least goatish of the comic journal's themes—from which fact I leave you to imagine the rest.

And yet even the comic journal at its worst, or the Nevsky Prospekt at its worst, would seem to the sincere, earnest and virtuous Russian to represent social sins of no moment compared with the transgressions that daily we commit and never think of. To the Russian conviction and conscientious practice a lack of hospitality is far more immoral than unsanctioned relations between the sexes. The guest has most sacred and inalienable rights; even the stranger within the gates cannot be viewed with indifference. It used to be the commonest experience for a traveler, if he were above the level of the tramp, to enter a village where he had never been before, and if the inn were crowded find exuberant welcome and entertainment at the best house in the place. Even the poorest was always sure of shelter and food. There was something like this in our Western country in the pioneer days, but in Russia it was universal and the spirit of it survives against all the hardening processes of civilization.

An American mining engineer, making a long and lonely journey in a sledge across remote Siberia, came into a considerable town one night and while waiting for his packs to be unstrapped fell into conversation with a resident. As soon as the local man discovered the nationality of the visitor nothing would do but that the Amerikansky must stay at the villager's house. With infinite labor and pains he cared for the visitor's baggage, led him into a really comfortable and clean abode and then inquired minutely concerning his taste in Russian delicacies. Some of these not being in the house, the host went out and ransacked the village for them. Wherever he went he had only to say that he was entertaining a traveler, a man from a far country, to have the best there was placed at his disposal. In the matter of drinks the American was beguiled into an admission that his fancy was ale, and the host managed to secure the only bottle of this restorative in the entire region, I suppose. It had been brought up the river to Krasnoyarsk by an English skipper, who, as an evidence of esteem, had presented it to a native by whom it was held in almost superstitious reverence. Yet it had to come forth at the news that a stranger from a far country was in town and wanted that little bottle to make him quite happy.

---

[11] There was an explosion of illustrated newspapers in 1917 with politically potent humorous drawings, many making fun of Nicholas and Alexandra.

Meantime his hosts made preparations to feed him, apparently under the impression, he said afterward, that his appetite had increased in proportion to his distance from home. The feast lasted the better part of the night and then, the poor man said pathetically, seemed to begin again. For just as he was congratulating himself that all was over, and, feeling stuffed like a sausage, was expecting a chance to get to bed, they brought out another table with another assortment of dainties, like ham and smoked goose, and commanded him to a final repast, being convinced that as he had eaten no more than what he deemed enough for six men he would perish before morning unless he now took a little something to sustain him.

And in the morning they all kissed him with great heartiness and prayed for blessings on him and came out to tuck him into his sledge like a baby and see that he was all wrapped up in furs and safe for his journey—and they never even mastered his name! They did not care. He was a stranger far from home, traveling alone, and the big, warm Russian heart went out to him.[12]

To fail of any possible kindness to him would have been their idea of immorality, and they would be perfectly honest and conscientious in that idea.

It is their strength and it is their weakness. The impracticable Bolshevik philosophy could never have gained foothold with them if it had not the appeal of universal federation, all the world to be made happy and all to be good friends and peaceful neighbors together. It was perfectly characteristic that having accepted this alluring dream of universal peace the Bolsheviks should be ready to go out and fight their countrymen for it. They were determined to have peace and loving brotherhood if they had to wade through blood to get it.

As I have before explained, the German propaganda understood this flawlessly, as it always masters whatever can be turned to its advantage, and when I was in Russia all of the German press agency and secret-manipulation work was done along these lines. It was the German play to represent that the masses of people everywhere, being downtrodden and oppressed by the capitalist class, were ready at a moments notice to arise and adopt the Bolshevik plan for the Instantaneous Millennium, the only thing necessary being that the Bolsheviks of Russia should lead the way. The German agents even diligently encouraged the belief that Germany was about to revolt and proclaim the German Republic! Germany, where there was as much chance of a Revolution as there was at the North Pole![13]

A lavish table, such as I have suggested in the story of the mining engineer, was always a feature of the life of the well-to-do Russian household. In plain terms, they were great eaters; I used to wonder at their storage capacity, which excelled anything

---

[12] This story he was told was likely greatly exaggerated, but affirmed his belief in Russian goodness.

[13] Again, he overstates German influence. Ironically, the very German revolt and republic came into being a year later.

of the kind I had ever observed. Yet a fat Russian is a rare spectacle. Germans eat a great deal and get fatty degeneration; Russians eat a great deal and keep within a reasonable girth. Not by exercise, God knows; the well-to-do Russian abhors it with all the vigor of a soul gifted in expression. He would not walk across the street if he could be carried, and his idea of rational existence is to sit at ease in a great chair into which he sinks half of his corporeal existence, to smoke an excellent cigarette of his nation's own devising, and to take part in voluble but often brilliant conversation. Upon the races that exult in rude sports, baseball, hockey, long hikes and the rest, he looks with wonder. He has neither contempt for them nor the least desire to imitate. He merely does not understand why they think they are having fun.

I am talking now of the ruling classes and their satellites under the old regime. With the peasants, of course, the case was different; there was small chance, as I have before indicated, that they would be overfed or grow atrophied for the lack of muscular exertion. Yet the peasants invariably looked well-nourished.[14] The truth is, that Bussia is normally a land of plenty and the climate demands calories and hearty food.

A dinner at the house of a Russian in easy circumstances is an affair of some moment; eating being in that climate the most important function of life, there is no disposition to take a light or frivolous view of a matter of such solemn significance. I believe the meal is never served on time, nor anywhere near the schedule; a fact so pleasantly remindful of the American railroad that when you think about it you feel quite comfortable and at home.[15] You enter the house on the ground floor and find first a large and rather bare reception-room with a huge fireplace and some comfortable seats near it. The purpose of this seems to be to give the guest in winter time a chance to thaw out and recover the use of his limbs, and in view of the kind of winters common in that part of the world the device is not only humane but necessary.

Then you go up an elaborate and wide staircase to the parlor and living-rooms, which are all above the first floor. These rooms are always fringed all the way around with chairs, placed against the wall and as thickly as may be, a custom said to have been originated by Peter the Great, who was a chairmaker himself and may have started the fashion for the sake of the trade. When at last, just before hope has become extinct and you inanimate, dinner is announced, you are led first of all to a small snow-white table in the corner of the dining-room, every inch of it crowded with dishes of food and with bottles. This is the celebrated sagusta or zakiska (like every other Russian word you can spell it any old way) upon which, a plate and a fork having been thrust into your hands, you are expected to make the attack while standing and conversing with your neighbor. There are radishes, pickles, salt and smoked fish,

---

[14] "Well-nourished" varied dramatically by time and place. There were periods and areas of starvation.

[15] A joke about the well-known frequency with which American railroads ran late.

sliced ham, sliced eggs, salads, sliced tomatoes and onions, various things you don't know the name of, and, in spite of prohibition, vodka and Scotch whisky.[16]

It takes about half an hour to tack your way over this ceremony, which is merely the harbor-bar to the full repast, and by that time the Occidental [Western] visitor feels that he has eaten a full meal, and cares for no more. But the Russian—he has had no more than an appetizer, a bracer, a cocktail, and now feels in fettle for the serious trencher work of the evening. So you sit down at the large table in the center of the room and there comes on first bortch or shtchi, a wondrous soup, unequaled in all the cooking of all the rest of the world, made either of shredded cabbage or shredded beets with other ingredients unknown to me but probably of celestial origin. With the first spoonful of this amazing concoction the most jaded appetite in the world will arise and demand more. Also, there comes a light, fluffy roll, filled with chopped meat or something, which you are expected to put into the soup and eat with it.

Next there will probably come sterlet, a long, slender fish that looks somewhat like a pickerel but is much better, and is served with a mysterious brown sauce. After that will be a roast, served with a dressing of buckwheat fixed up in some occult way to cause you to overeat of it, and potatoes. Then, served as a separate course, round, fresh cucumbers, most excellent, and the rest of the dinner, salad, dessert and coffee, will be much of the regular European style; except the cheese, which is a Russian specialty and a thing apart, and the pastry, which will be unlike any of your previous acquaintance. Also, there will be (spite of prohibition again) some excellent claret from the Crimea, and other wines aplenty.

About three hours will be consumed in working through this bill of fare. And in about an hour and a half more you will be expected to start on another.

The conversation, meantime, will have been of an unusual order of merit. Except France, I suppose there is no other country where the average of table-talk is so high as in Russia among the educated; and it will be carried on in about all the languages of civilization, for the Russian is by nature the world's first polyglot; he takes to languages as a Norwegian takes to the sea. At your table there will probably be not a Russian that cannot speak at least five languages, and speak them fluently and accurately.[17] It is a point of politeness with the educated Russian to speak the language of his visitor. I have had Russians address me in purest American. One of my neighbors at a dinner table said "nothing doing" and "the once-over" and talked about rubber-necks, boobs and things that got his goat like a native of our most exclusive strain, a delicate attention to which I am sure the heart of any American would have warmed.

When, after another repast, hardly less formidable than the first, you are allowed to go home, not altogether free from the fear of apoplexy, if the season is midsummer

---

[16] Russia technically had been on alcohol prohibition since the outbreak of war in 1914.

[17] He is describing the very aristocratic class, although well educated Russians often spoke 2–4 foreign languages.

you will go by daylight even if the hour be midnight, and it will probably be all of that. Automobiles being few and hard to come by, you will be conveyed in a funny little go-cart, not much bigger than babies have in Brooklyn, with a low seat behind and a high seat in front whereon is perched a grotesque figure that looks as if he were expressly made up for a good buffo part in a comic opera.

This is the cabman. He has on his head a low crowned stiff hat with a broad brim much turned up at the sides, and he wears a vast blue overcoat that stretches from his chin to his heels. No matter how hot the weather may be—and July sees blistering days in Petrograd—he wears this monstrous garment closely buttoned to the top. You would as reasonably expect him to wear earmuffs and have a foot-warmer. But that is not all. The whole center region of this most preposterous garment, beginning above the waistline, and extending all the way around, is thickly padded and quilted, so that he must be wearing there the equivalent of about six thicknesses of the heavy cloth of which the coat is made. You would think the man would perish; you would think he would dissolve and flow down the street, a stream of molten fat. Yet on the hottest day of July when you are panting along in your Palm Beach suit and hunting the shade, he will sit in the sun in that mass of quilts and things and never seem in the least perturbed.

You will probably notice that this driver person knows comparatively little about the city and has difficulty in finding his way. That is because he is a peasant that comes here to drive when work is slack on the farm. You will also notice that he will pay no attention to tariffs but conduct his transportation business on the good old principle of what the traffic will bear or what he thinks he can extract from you, which must on the average be a pretty fair sum, for some of the choicest stories current in Petrograd relate to the wealth of the cabmen.

But all of this evening's entertainment, you must remember, pertains to the world of the fortunate. You went out to dine with a rich Russian, very likely a large landowner, or a manufacturer, a man with a title, for the Russian nobility never had the least objection to going into profitable trade. It is a very different story when you drop below that stratum. There never was a country where these strata distinctions were more sharply marked than in Russia under the old system; there never was one where waste of life was more wanton or more profligate—wasted by the fortunate in idling and stuffing, wasted by the vast hordes of common population in an existence without hope or light. After the counter-revolution of October, 1917, Americans became so disgusted with the Bolsheviks they forgot the conditions that produced Bolsheviks and made a Bolshevik day inevitable. Yet it is wholesome for us to be reminded of the fact and to dwell upon it, that the Russian people were brought by their Revolution out of intense darkness into sudden light, and that for a time there was necessarily groping around after the impossible. We seemed to have acquired a knowledge of history without its philosophy. On a calm review it will seem that what happened was but normal.

THE INFLUENCE OF MANNERS AND MORALS

As to the intensity of the darkness, let me recall one or two little records that may serve to make it seem real to us.

In 1910 the medical profession of Russia revealed the startling fact that there was in proportion to population far more neurasthenia in Russia than in any other country in the world, and it was not, as is generally the case elsewhere, confined to the more fortunate among the people; in Russia it prevailed most among the peasants and the toilers. Why among them? Because, said the doctors, the weight of the gloom and horrors in which they lived lowered their nervous vitality and made them prone to this disease as to many others.

Russia, in those days, also led all the world in the proportion of its suicides. Most amazing and impressive fact of all, among the suicides was a cruel number of the young. Russia was the only country on earth where little children killed themselves. Not all the speech of all the earth could produce an arraignment of the system more tremendous or more eloquent than that; the only country on earth where little children deliberately killed themselves. A few years before the Revolution came with its blessed light the suicides among children had become so numerous and so terrifying that a government commission was appointed to investigate the causes and find remedies, and this commission busied itself in organizing among the pupils in the public schools anti-suicide societies that it might stop the growth of an appalling evil. In two years forty-five children of less than fourteen years are said to have destroyed themselves in Moscow alone.

And why did they destroy themselves?

Because, according to the commission, they were overwhelmed with the distress, the melancholy and the hopelessness around them. They arrived at years where they could gain one competent glimpse of life as it really was in Russia. It gloomed before them, a weary struggle without the joy of liberty, without a moment free from the black shadow of the seven-times-accursed system that weighed down the hearts of all men about them. It was enough. They preferred death. "I have nothing to live for," wrote a girl ten years old. Then she stabbed herself. I should think the dagger she used wrote an indictment of autocracy that will never be returned as satisfied so long as there is an autocrat left upon this earth.

And for my part I think I can manage to be fairly patient with whatever vagaries or illusions the new-born democracy of Russia may indulge in while it is finding itself and reaching its eventual sure anchorage of permanency. At least it does not blacken with despair the lives of the people it governs; it does not drive little children to commit suicide.[18]

---

[18] A widespread problem of the time, and not just in Russia.

Index

Adler, Frederick, 22
Alexandrieff, Father, 54
Alexeev, General, 117
Allies (Allied Governments), ix, 4, 10, 11, 13, 14, 15, 16, 17, 18, 20, 24, 29, 41, 73, 85
All-Russian Congress of Soviets of Workers' and Soldiers' Deputies, ix, x, 17, 18, 27, 28, 29, 30, 32, 33, 34, 35, 37, 38, 39, 41, 42, 50, 91, 92, 120, 124
Alsace and Lorraine, 11
Aleutian Islands, 83
Alexander II Museum of Modern Russian Art, 135
American Orchestra and Theodore Thomas, The, viii
American Mission, 12, 17, 18, 47
American Revolution, 107
Amsterdam, 6
Anarchists (Anarchism), 6, 25, 36, 37, 40, 46
Anglo-Saxon, 23, 38, 99, 131
Archangel, 72
Arctic Circle, 24, 66, 87
Argentina, 25
Austria (Austrian), 22, 23, 95, 121
Azef, Yevno, 65

Baltic, 24
Bastile (Bastille), 57, 58
Battalion of Death, 86, 93, 95, 96
beer, 5
Belgium (Belgians), 122
Berlin, 8, 10, 135
Bismarckism (Bismarck), 8
Black Hundreds, 67
Black Sea Fleet, 46, 126
Bloody Sunday (1905), xi, 25, 58, 87
Bolsheviks, xi, 15, 19, 34, 36, 37, 40, 41, 42, 51, 57, 69, 84, 85, 96, 98, 112, 113, 114, 115, 116, 124, 125, 127, 136, 140
Botchkareva, Maria, xi, 94
Breshkovskaya, Catherine, 49

Brest-Litvosk, Treaty of, 14, 114
Buriats, 44, 82

Cadetsky Corpus, 18, 27, 28
Caligula, 56
Cape Nome, 22
Carpathians, 117
Causasus, 15
Chelmsford Abbey, England, 23
Chernov, Victor, 122
China (Chinese), 82
Chita, 93
Chkheidze, Nikolai, ix, 29, 38, 118
Christiana, 6
Civil War (US), 47
Clay, General Cassius M., 47, 127
Comstock, Anthony, 135
Constitutional Democratic Party (Cadets), 36
Copenhagen, 6
Cossacks, 46, 59, 82
Crimea, 31, 100, 139
Cuba, 11

Davenport, Iowa, viii
Desmoulins, C., 29
Dry Tortugas, 22
Duma, 29, 30, 59, 120

Eastern China Railroad Company, 79
Eastern Siberian, 79
Egypt, 68
Ems, 8
English Liberal, 50

Fall of the Romanovs, The, viii
Far Cathay, 8
February Revolution, xi, 3, 21
Field of Mars, 12, 19, 28, 42, 67
Fifth Avenue, 99
Figner, Vera, 90

Finance, Minister of, 16
Fiske, John, 107
Fleurot, Arnot Dosch, 6
Foreign Affairs, Minister of, 41
France (French), 8, 13, 66, 91, 99
France, Anatole, 8
Francis, David R., vii
French Revolution, 113

Gentile, 54
George, Lloyd, 37
Germany (Germans), ix, 4, 6–9, 11, 12, 18, 20, 26, 38, 46, 51, 53, 55, 59, 67, 68, 69, 82, 83, 85, 92, 96, 116, 118, 121, 122, 124, 130, 136
Glennon, Admiral James H., 47
Gobi Desert, 82
"God Save the Tsar," 26
Gorky, Maxim, 128, 129, 130
Gregorian Calendar, xi
Great Britain (British), 8, 13, 17, 32, 38, 53, 122, 128

Harbin, 81, 82
Harriman, E. H., 80
Harte, Bret, 132
Hindoos, 82
Hottentot, 50
House of Commons, 38

intelligentsia, 24
Italy, 11, 99
Irkutsk, 66

Jacobite, 66
Japan (Japanese), 58, 73, 75, 77, 82, 122
Jefferson, Thomas, 37, 49, 50
Jericho, 114
Jews, 54, 120
Joan of Arc, 88
Judas, 96
Julian Calendar, xi

Kautsky K., 28
Kazan Cathedral, 127
Kerensky, A., 35, 40, 41
Kishinev, 120
Korea (Koreans), 82
Krasnoyarsk, 136

Kronstadt, 46, 57, 58, 59, 60
Kropotkin, P., 14
Krupps, 9
Kurgesi, 82
Kuril Islands, 83

Lake Baikal, x, 75, 77
Lassalle, F., 28
Left, 13, 36
Lena River, 31, 66, 118
Lenin, V. I., 34, 35
Levolf, 102
Liteinia, 88
London, 104, 131
Lvov, Prince G., 70

Macaulay, Thomas Babington, 128
Machias, 8
Manchuria, 75, 82, 83
Marne, The, 10
Mars, 35
"Marsellaise," 26
Marx, Karl, 29
Maximalists, 36, 124
Mensheviks, 36, 98, 114, 125, 127
Michael, Grand Duke, 55
Mid-Siberian, 79
Miliukov, P., 15
Miller, Henry, 84
Minimalists, 36, 114
Mir, 108, 110
Moltkes, 9
Mongolia (Mongolians), 82
Morskaia River, 67
Moscow, x, 45, 54, 71, 72, 73, 104, 106, 141
Moscow Union of Consumers' Societies, 104
Moses, 16, 117
Mrs. Warren's Profession, 134
Mukden, 75
Munich, 135

Napoleon, 16, 41
National Assembly of Revolutionary France, 29
National Association for the Advancement of Colored People, viii
National Council, 17
National Soviet, 7
Neva River, 27, 93

INDEX

Nevsky Prospekt, 67, 87, 88, 131, 132, 136
New Day, 13, 19, 38
New York, vii, viii, 129, 130
New York Board of Alderman, 31
nihilists, 4
North American Indian, 83, 122
North Dakota, 83
North Pole, 66, 137
Norwegian, 139
Nova Zembla, 8
Novaia Zhizn, 130

Oates, Titus, 65
Occidental, 139
Odessa, 106, 126
Oxford, 42
Oriental, 117, 120, 132

Park Lane, 99
Passing Point Number 37, 21, 24
Pekin, 77, 82
People's Liberty Party, 36
People's Socialist Party, 36
Perovskaia, Sophie, 89
Peter and Paul Fortress, 55
Peter the Great, 138
Petrograd (St. Petersburg), vii, x, 6, 7, 9, 14, 25, 27, 29, 30, 31, 32, 41, 42, 45, 46, 51, 52, 53, 55, 57, 60, 68, 71, 72, 73, 75, 77, 80, 81, 84, 87, 88, 90, 92, 93, 94, 95, 106, 113, 114, 118, 123, 124, 140
Petrograd Soldiers' and Workers' Congress, 39
Petrograd Soviet, ix
Philippines, 11
Piccadilly, 131
Platon, Archbishop of Petrograd, 95
Plekhanov, G., 14
Polosk, 102
Posts, Minister of, 40
Potemkin, 58, 125, 126
Provisional Government, vii, x, 59, 69, 84, 109
Puerto Rico, 11
Pulitzer Prize, viii
Pullman, 76
Puritan, 132

Rabinovitch, Lydia, 91

Railroads, Minister of, 16
Rasputin, G., 54, 132, 133, 136
Red Flag, 25
Red Leary's Toughs, 33
Reign of Terror, 113
Revolution of 1905, 86, 106, 119
Right, 34
Roman Empire, 68
Romanoff, Alexander (Alexander II), 75, 89
Romanoff, Alexander (Alexander III), 75
Romanoff, Nicholas (Nicholas I), 74–75
Romanoff, Nicholas (Nicholas II), 33, 54, 63, 87
Roosevelt, Theodore, vii
Rubles, 72, 104, 105
Russell, Charles Edward, vii–xi
Russian Orthodox Church, 53
Russian (Bolshevik) Revolution, x, 7, 10, 11, 12, 19, 20, 21, 23, 31, 34, 37, 44, 46, 49, 50, 52, 53, 54, 56, 57, 58, 60, 62, 64, 65, 67, 69, 71, 74, 82, 88, 89, 90, 93, 97, 104, 105, 107, 111, 112, 118, 121, 123, 132, 133, 137

Sandhurst, 8
San Francisco, 54
sans culotte, 113
Sault Ste. Marie, Michigan, 76
Savings, Loan, and Credit Associations, 104
Scandihoovian, 82
Sebastopol, 46
Serbia (Serbians), 99, 122
Sergius, Grand Duke, 65
serfdom, xi, 97, 105, 107, 108
Shaw, George Bernard, 134
Shepherd, William G., 6
Siamese, 13
Siberia, x, 21, 22, 24, 26, 32, 37, 40, 44, 48, 50, 52, 55, 63, 65, 66, 74, 80, 82, 89, 90, 91, 104, 123, 136
Skobelev, Mikhail, ix, 70, 122
Social Democratic Party, 36
Social(ist) Revolutionist (Revolutionary) Party, 36, 50
Socialists, vii, viii, 115, 116
Soviets, ix
Soviet of Sailors' and Workers' Deputies, 59
Spiridonova, Maria, xi, 51, 52, 53, 90, 92
Stockholm, 6, 7

St. George's Cross and Medal, 94
St. Isacc's Cathedral, 95
St. Johnsbury, Vermont, 23
Stevens, John F., 84
Sweden, 67
Switzerland, 99

Tannenberg, Battle of, 83
Tereshchenko, M., 41, 42
Thomas, Albert, 117
Tobolsk, 108
Tomolsk, 102
Trans-Baikal, 79
Trans-Siberian Railroad, x, 21, 73, 74, 75, 78, 79, 80, 81, 82, 85, 93
Trentino, 11
Trieste, 11
Trinity Church, viii
Trotsky, Leon, ix, 35
Troubetskoy, Prince Paul, 110
Trudoviks, 114, 127
Tsar (Tsarism), 5, 13, 14, 19, 20, 22, 23, 25, 26, 28, 29, 44, 54, 55, 57, 62, 63, 66, 75, 78, 79, 81, 98, 107, 110, 111, 124, 126, 133
Tsereteli, Irakli, ix, 35, 40, 118, 122
Tuberculosis, 101
Turkey (Turks), 82, 120

Udinsk, 82
Union of Creameries Associations, 104
universal education, 6
universal suffrage, 6, 31, 32
Ural, 79
Utopia, 4, 135

Vladivostok, 21, 24, 73, 75, 77, 78, 79, 80, 81, 82, 123
Vodka, 4, 5, 100
Volga River, 75, 78
von Bernstorff, Ambassador, 7, 18

War Building, 25
War, Minister of, 41
Washington, DC, 7, 18, 59
West Point, 8, 27
Western Siberian, 79
Wilson, Woodrow, vii, viii, 43
Winch, 82

Winter Palace, 25, 27, 84, 87, 88
Witte, Count Sergei, 119, 120

Yacht Club, 32
Yenesei River, 78

Zakiska, 138
Zemstvos, 109, 110

www.ingramcontent.com/pod-product-compliance
Lightning Source LLC
Chambersburg PA
CBHW032027230426
43671CB00005B/227